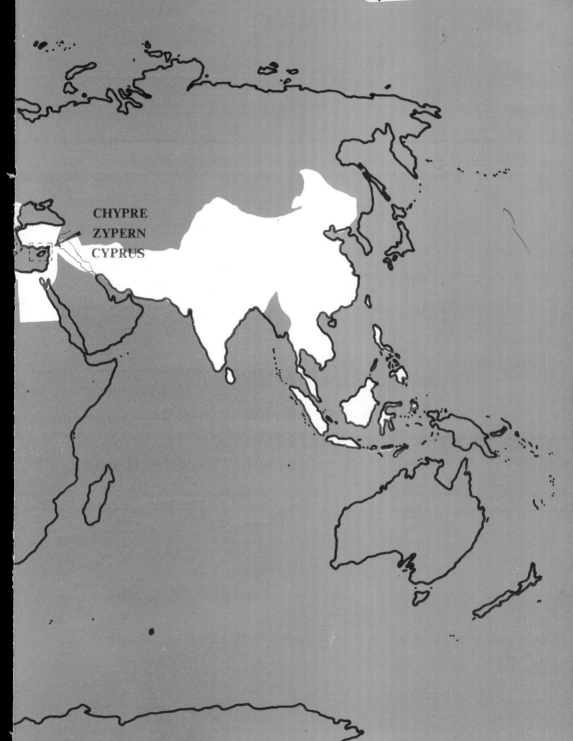

CHYPRE
ZYPERN
CYPRUS

MEXICO	Jacques Soustelle
PERSIA I (From the origins to the Achaemenids)	Jean-Louis Huot, Agrégé of the University; Member of the French Institute of Archaeology of Beirut
PERSIA II (From the Seleucids to the Sassanians)	Vladimir Lukonin, Curator at the Hermitage Museum, Leningrad
PERU	Rafael Larco Hoyle †, Director of the Rafael Larco Herrera Museum, Lima
PREHISTORY	Denise de Sonneville-Bordes, Ph. D.
ROME	Gilbert Picard, Professor at the Sorbonne, Paris
SOUTH CAUCASUS	Boris B. Piotrovsky, Director of the Hermitage Museum, Leningrad
SOUTH SIBERIA	Mikhail Gryaznov, Professor at the Archaeological Institute of Leningrad
SYRIA-PALESTINE I (Ancient Orient)	Jean Perrot, Head of the French Archaeological Mission in Israel
SYRIA-PALESTINE II (Classical Orient)	Michael Avi Yonah, Professor at the Hebrew University of Jerusalem
THE TEUTONS	R. Hachmann, Professor at the University of Saarbrücken
URARTU	Boris B. Piotrovsky, Director of the Hermitage Museum, Leningrad

ANCIENT CIVILIZATIONS

Series prepared under the direction of
Jean Marcadé, Professor of Archaeology
at the University of Bordeaux

THE ANCIENT CIVILIZATION OF

CYPRUS

VASSOS KARAGEORGIS

122 illustrations in colour; 59 illustrations in black and white

COWLES EDUCATION CORPORATION

488, MADISON AVENUE

NEW YORK, N.Y. 10022

CONTENTS

PREFACE

*W*ithin the vast territory of the Eastern Mediterranean, an area of such outstanding archaeological richness and importance, Cyprus is coming to occupy an increasingly prominent place. The significance of the island in early times and the distinctive quality of its output require no further demonstration; and it is no longer possible to regard Cyprus as a mere offshoot of Aegean civilisation or as no more than a staging point in the commercial and cultural expansion of the ancient Near East. The achievements of the Late Bronze Age and the Archaic period in Cyprus would be sufficient in themselves to justify a special volume in the "Archaeologia Mundi" series; and yet these are no more than the most brilliant chapters in the long history of the island, which—even if we confine our attention to ancient times—has had its full share of vicissitudes, its alternation of decline and resurgence.

But there are other reasons too. Since it is the object of this series to introduce its readers to the diverse aspects of contemporary archaeology in all its range and variety, Cyprus cannot be excluded from our survey. It is one of the areas where archaeologists—both local scholars and foreign expeditions—are most actively at work, vying with one another in friendly rivalry; and the exemplary organisation, rigorous scientific method and technical ingenuity which have been displayed here have been rewarded by some sensational discoveries, particularly at Enkomi and Salamis.

We are particularly grateful to Professor Vassos Karageorghis for undertaking to present to our readers the problems, the methods and the results of Cypriote archaeology, to which he himself has contributed so much. This book, with its clear arrangement of the material and its wealth of illustrations, is a magnificent introduction to the great range of treasures which archaeology has revealed in Cyprus.

J. M.

We should like to express our sincere gratitude to His Beatitude Archbishop Makarios, President of the Republic of Cyprus, for his interest and support throughout the preparation of this work.

Our thanks are also due to Mr Patroclos Stavrou, Under Secretary of State on the staff of the President of the Republic of Cyprus, who has given us every possible assistance.

Finally the author would like to say a word of particular thanks to Col. J. S. Last, F.S.A., for his valuable help.

INTRODUCTION

Cyprus, lying on the periphery of two great cultural regions, the Aegean and the Near East, was soon discovered by students of both these cultures, and the study of its archaeology and history became a necessity for both the classicist and the orientalist. For many years, however, this study was only incidental to other investigations, and sometimes it was extremely superficial. The archaeology of Cyprus was unfortunate in being exposed for so long to the attentions of amateurs and treasure-hunters. Unlike Crete, where the sensational discoveries by Evans aroused world-wide interest and attracted serious archaeologists and students, Cyprus attracted looters and amateur diggers whose object was to build up private collections, either for their own pleasure or for profit. And certainly the soil of Cyprus has produced great quantities of ancient objects, though not all of them can claim artistic merit.

This, together with the lack of real scholarly interest, kept the island out of the limelight of archaeological research. Even those few scholars who became interested in Cyprus were moved by curiosity rather than by any real scientific impulse.

It was only in the second quarter of this century that scholars discovered the archaeology of Cyprus as a separate study in itself. Superstitions inherited from the past had to be overcome; but now a handful of pioneers boldly laid the foundations for the study of the island's past. The monumental work of the Swedish Cyprus Expedition, both in the field and in their publications, marked an epoch. Scholars of many nations have made Cyprus a special field of research, and every year the number of specialists in this field is increasing. But whereas the scientific world has at its disposal the full excavation reports and the specialised studies produced by many scholars in various languages, the ordinary intelligent layman and even the scholar who specialises in regions outside the Eastern Mediterranean often finds difficulty, owing to the lack of a convenient source of reliable information, in gaining a general picture of the archaeology of

Cyprus. Anyone undertaking to produce an adequate manual of Cypriote archaeology should, ideally, have a thorough knowledge of the subject over a period of more than six thousand years; and though the present writer does not claim such erudition he welcomed the opportunity to offer the fruit of his fifteen years of experience in the archaeology of Cyprus, in spite of pressing obligations in the field and in administration. The reader is introduced in this book to the problems which Cypriote archaeology has faced in the past and continues to face at present, and to the methods now being applied to raise it to a reputable standard. Finally this book contains a broad outline of the archaeology of Cyprus from the Neolithic period down to the end of the Roman period, emphasising the most characteristic results of modern research for each period. The specialist may find dogmatic generalisations about certain controversial aspects of the archaeology of Cyprus. In his defence the author must plead limitations of space and the character of the book. It may be objected, for example, that there is some inequality in the treatment of the various archaeological periods and sites. While this may be partly due to unevenness in the author's knowledge, it must also be emphasised that there are certain periods and sites which are outstanding, for example the Mycenaean period at Enkomi and Kition, and the archaic period at Salamis.

Chapters I and II have been much influenced in their general layout by Professor Platon's book on Crete in the same series. In Chapter II, however, on the Methods, we have omitted those methods which are common to all archaeological regions, e.g., stratigraphic observation, photography, preservation techniques, etc. We have mentioned only matters which in some degree are peculiar to Cyprus, or methods which, so far as we know, have not been described elsewhere. In this chapter, too, we have taken for granted that the reader is familiar with the principles of archaeological techniques as described by Platon. The third chapter, on the Results, is much longer than the other two. We had, however, to cover a period of more than six thousand years, and at least the highlights had to be described at some length. More space has been given to excavations hitherto unpublished elsewhere.

V. K.

MAPS

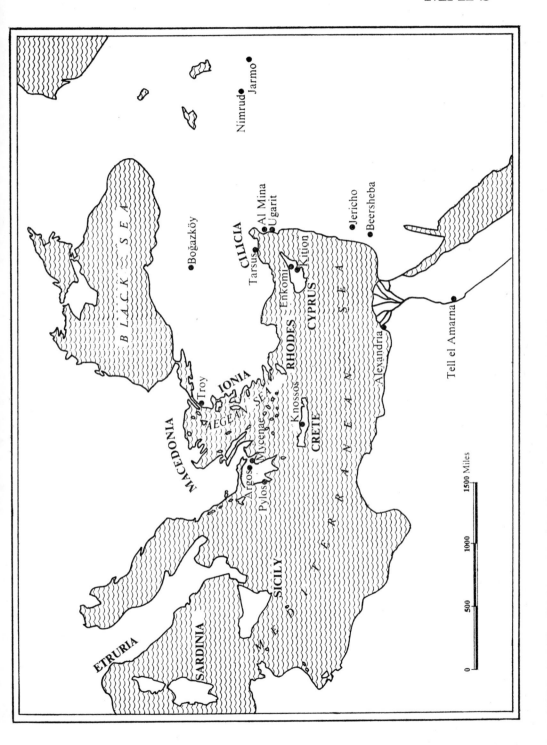

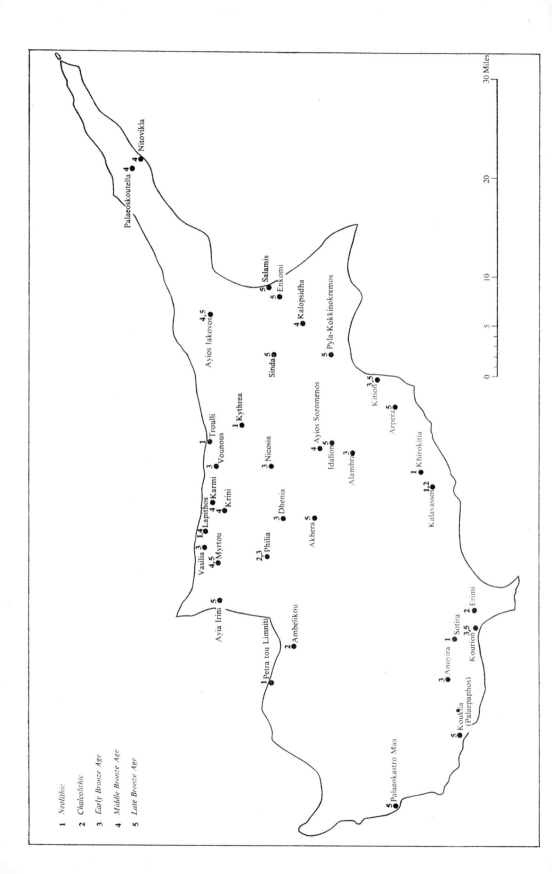

1 Neolithic
2 Chalcolithic
3 Early Bronze Age
4 Middle Bronze Age
5 Late Bronze Age

5 Nitovikla

4 Palaeoskoutella

4,5 Ayios Iakovos

5 Salamis
5 Enkomi
4 Kalopsidha

5 Pyla-Kokkinokremos

Sinda **5**

Kition **3,5**

1 Kythrea
Arpera **5**

Troulli **1**
Vounous **3**
1 Khirokitia

Krini **4**
3 Nicosia
4 Ayios Sozomenos
5
Idalion **5**
Alambra **3**
1,2
Kalavassos
● Karmi
Lapithos **1,4**
3 Dhenia
Vasilia **3**
Akhera **5**
4,5 Myrtou

Philia **2,3**

Ayia Irini **5**

Ambelikou **2**

Petra tou Limniti **1**

Anoyira **1**
Sotira
Kourion **3,5**
Erimi **2**

Kouklia **3**
(Palaepaphos)

5 Palaeokastro Maa

0   5   10   20   30 Miles

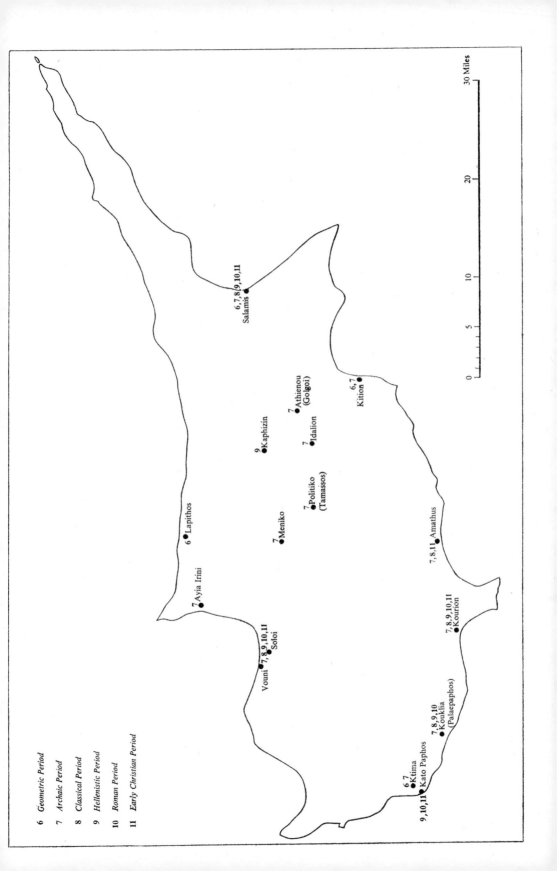

6   Geometric Period
7   Archaic Period
8   Classical Period
9   Hellenistic Period
10 Roman Period
11 Early Christian Period

30 Miles

6,7,8,9,10,11
Salamis

6,7
Kition

7 Athienou
  (Golgoi)

9 Kaphizin

7 Idalion

7 Politiko
  (Tamassos)

6 Lapithos

7 Meniko

7 Ayia Irini

7,8,11 Amathus

Vouni 7,8,9,10,11
       Soloi

7,8,9,10,11
Kourion

7,8,9,10
Kouklia
(Palaepaphos)

6,7
Ktima
Kato Paphos

9,10,11

THE PROBLEMS

I

Changing Views on the Antiquities of Cyprus

The Centuries of Neglect

The Arab invasions of the 7th century A.D. completed the destruction of the ancient cities of Cyprus, which had begun three centuries earlier as a result of repeated earthquakes *(Plates 1–7)*. New towns were built, often near the site of the old; but this meant an end of antiquity both chronologically and physically. Salamis—a characteristic example—having been the capital of the island for more than fifteen centuries, was abandoned in flames. Thick layers of ashes and burnt sandstone revealed during the recent excavations bear silent testimony to its tragic fall. Violent north-easterly winds blew the sand from the southern shores of the Karpass peninsula, covering the massive walls of its ruined palaces and public buildings.

This wilderness of fallen walls and broken columns *(Plates 4, 5)*, combined with the romantic echo of the ancient names of the towns which had been preserved, enchanted the mediaeval travellers—the first intellectuals to visit Cyprus for many centuries, mainly from Europe[1]. Most of them, scholars and pious men, evoked the splendour of the ancient cities through their knowledge of the ancient Greek and Latin authors and the Bible. Salamis was looked upon as the foundation of Teucer, of St Barnabas, of St Catherine and of St Epiphanios. It was with the enigmas of these naked ruined cities of the comparatively recent past that the interest in the archaeology of Cyprus began. The Swiss pilgrim Jodicus de Meggen, who visited Cyprus in 1542, was greatly impressed by the ruins of Salamis, where, he wrote, "there remain, to this day, enormous stones strewn about the place, and great masses of ruins. There may be seen today arches of aqueducts raised high aloft, though for the most part they are eaten away by age or completely collapsed. The power and resources of Salamis may be gauged even now since, when the ground is dug up and monuments and tombs laid open, innumerable and precious pieces of jewellery are brought to light, such as golden and silver necklaces, rings, gems and other ornaments of great price. These things are discovered by sieving the earth and observing it very carefully. For it was the custom in early times that the dead should be buried adorned with ornaments of this kind. We saw with our own eyes that this must have been so, for we went down ourselves into the subterranean crypts to visit those who were digging there; and we bought from them, sometimes with gold, sometimes with silver, various tokens of extreme antiquity; I would mention especially some exceedingly old coins, some of them of gold and some of bronze, embossed with both Greek and Latin characters"[2].

This picture must have been universal in the island. Stone robbers, roaming in the unprotected ruins, became also tomb-robbers, especially in a poverty-stricken and foreign-occupied country. Later, three hundred years of Turkish occupation offered ideal conditions for treasure-hunting, first by needy Cypriote peasants, and then increasingly by foreigners who might have either the curiosity of a scholar or the mania and cupidity of a collector. Thus the first contact with Cypriote antiquities was an unrestrained onslaught on the remains of the past.

The Awakening of Scholarly Interest

In the first half of the nineteenth century the first scholars began to express their opinions on the relics of the past which were being extracted from the soil of Cyprus—mainly the inscriptions and the coins[3]. The Duc Honoré Albert de Luynes bought a collection of Cypriote antiquities, which found its way to the Cabinet des Médailles in the Bibliothèque Nationale, Paris. The chance discovery at Idalion of a long text in the Cypriote syllabic script on a bronze tablet, eventually bought by the Duc de Luynes, initiated a lively interest in these "caractères inconnus", and the duke himself produced in 1 \}5′ the first scholarly book on Cypriote anti-quities, entitled *Numismatique et inscriptions cypriotes*. Epigraphy was a favourite subject with European classical scholars, and more familiar as a field of research than other aspects of the antiquities of Cyprus. This interest was maintained for nearly half a century, and culminated in the last quarter of the nineteenth century in the decipherment of the script. This was the first important step forward in the study of Cypriote archaeo-logy.

During the second half of the 19th century, while the interest of the scholar, especially the epigraphist, continued, a new element made its appearance on the scene of Cypriote archaeology, in the form of the amateur digger. Diplomats and bankers vied with one another in excavating for treasures, and it was during this period that the worst damage was done to Cypriote antiquities. This section would be incomplete without a reference to one of the most remarkable of these scholarly looters. Luigi Palma di Cesnola, an Italian-American, fought in Europe and in the American Civil War, after which he was breveted Brigadier-General and appointed U.S. consul in Cyprus (1865–77). During his period of office on the island he exploited his opportunities to the full and acquired by excavation and purchase, directly or indirectly, a vast collection of antiquities from all over the island. The New York Metropolitan Museum purchased his collection in 1872, and he was director of the Museum from 1879 until his death in 1904. It is idle to speculate on what would have been the fate of his acqui-sitions if he had not collected them, or on the effect of the public interest aroused by the Museum's display of Cyprus antiquities; one can but deplore the removal from its place of origin, without any proper scientific record, of such a great quantity of valuable, and often unique, scientific material. Cesnola's attributions of provenance seem to be reasonably correct, but his accounts of his so-called "discoveries" reflect the romantic attitude of his time towards such matters and betray his own conveniently vivid imagination to ᵢ extent which renders them scientifically valueless[4].

A German amateur archaeologist, Max Ohnefalsch-Richter, who also undertook excavations throughout the island on behalf of foreign museums and individuals, could on occasion achieve a proper scholarly standard, but by dint of his considerable erudition rather than by the scientific method he displayed in his work[5]. The same may be said of a British Museum expedition which excavated in various parts of the island from 1890 to 1896[6]. What was lacking was a scientific approach to excavation and a correct interpretation of stratigraphical phenomena, and above all a true knowledge of Cypriote antiquities, especially the pottery.

The Development of Scientific Method

The scholar who first tried to remedy these shortcomings was Sir John Myres. Faced with the problem of compiling a catalogue of the antiquities which Cesnola had sold to the Metropolitan Museum of New York, he was the first to try to classify the objects typologically and chronologically; he carried out stratigraphic excavations on the island, and by proper scientific observation established a chronological sequence in Cypriote archaeology which became a working standard for other scholars who followed him. Some sort of order was achieved, especially with regard to prehistoric antiquities, which had been for many years an inexplicable enigma[7].

The ground was, therefore, well prepared for the Swedish Cyprus Expedition, whose work from 1927 to 1930 laid solid foundations for Cypriote archaeology of all periods. Gjerstad's genius and erudition widened the horizons of Cyprus prehistory[8]. The first Neolithic remains on the island were revealed. The Bronze Age was subdivided in the light of careful stratigraphic observations. Cypriote antiquities were classified in detail and compared with those of the Aegean and the Near East. From now on it was possible to speak of Cypriote archaeology as a science. The excavation of settlements, palaces and fortresses, "temples" and tombs, enriched our knowledge of Cypriote architecture and religious and public

6, 7

9

life. The art of Cyprus in general can be now studied against its historical background, and its aesthetic study gives it a place in the history of art.

The Swedish Cyprus Expedition carried out an overall survey of Cypriote archaeology, and the publications which followed the excavations constitute the first scientific literature on the subject[9].

The work of C. F. A. Schaeffer[10], of P. Dikaios[11] and other individual scholars dealt very successfully with particular periods or special aspects of Cypriote archaeology, elaborating or correcting the work of the Swedish scholars[12]. Cypriote prehistory received the limelight for a long period, admittedly at the expense of later periods; and with the application of strict stratigraphic methods and the latest scientific techniques (chemical analysis and carbon 14 dating) it became one of the best known prehistoric periods in the Near East. The thorough exploration of Late Cypriote sites like Enkomi contributed also to the better knowledge of a period which is of crucial importance for the study of the later historical development of Cyprus, and to a better understanding of the art and archaeology of the Near East and the Aegean in general. New problems have emerged as a result of these excavations, for instance the origin and nature of the prehistoric Cypriote (Cypro-Minoan) script, which still remains undeciphered; but at the same time many other problems have been solved. Cyprus occupies a prominent place in the pattern of Near Eastern prehistoric studies, and scholars frequently use the results already attained in the study of Cypriote prehistory in order to interpret or date phenomena in the prehistory of other countries of the Near East.

A new angle of approach has been adopted since the independence of Cyprus in 1960. The emphasis is now on the sites of the cities of Cyprus: Salamis, Paphos, Kourion, Soloi, Palaepaphos. The excavations of the last forty years have enriched the museums of Europe, the United States and Cyprus with properly excavated antiquities which can be studied scientifically. Interest in the archaeology of Cyprus has been renewed during the last decade as a result of the new work in the field of Mycenaean and Homeric studies, in which Cyprus offers wide scope for research. The archaeology of Cyprus is now accorded a proper scientific status, and not only is it studied today by a great number of specialists, but in some universities it is taught as a special subject. This position has not been achieved without some losses and sacrifices. A factor which has greatly contributed to the survival of Cypriote archaeology is its apparently inexhaustible supply of study material. The peculiarities of the island's prehistoric material, and its crucial position between East and West from the Mycenaean period onwards, make the study of its archaeology a lively and challenging subject for the orientalist and the classicist alike.

Neolithic Beginnings

Difficulties of Chronology

The thorough investigations and the island-wide survey by Professor Gjerstad brought evidence as early as 1926 for a pre-Bronze Age culture in Cyprus, known as Neolithic. He was able to distinguish an early phase of this culture, represented on the small island of Petra tou Limniti, and characterised by the absence of pottery; and a second phase, with pottery, represented by sites at Lapithos and Kythrea. In fact Gjerstad described the first phase as pre-Neolithic, but later investigations elsewhere have demonstrated that the earliest culture hitherto discovered in Cyprus must be classified as Neolithic.

It has not yet been possible to trace any Palaeolithic or Mesolithic remains in Cyprus. We cannot exclude the possibility of their existence, especially when we consider that even the very earliest phase of the Neolithic culture (Neolithic I) is widely distributed throughout the island, and new settlements are being recorded on the map every year. This widespread and highly developed early cultural stage may have evolved from an earlier more primitive stage, but the problem is to trace remains of this stage; so far none have been identified. The discovery in recent years of pre-Neolithic cultures in Anatolia and Palestine may be indicative and encouraging for those engaged in the search for earlier remains of the island's first culture.

The most extensive excavations of Neolithic sites and the general investigation and study of this period were undertaken by P. Dikaios from 1936 onwards. The main site which he excavated was Khirokitia *(Plates 11-12)*, where two cultural phases were recognised, Neolithic I (without pottery) and Neolithic II (with pottery). According to the first estimate the earliest settlement at Khirokitia was dated to c. 4000 B.C., but carbon 14 tests made in 1955 place the pre-pottery culture of Khirokitia at c. 5800. Neolithic II, which has been recognised at other sites such as Sotira and Kalavassos as well as at Khirokitia, is dated by carbon 14 to c. 3500. If we consider that the end of Neolithic I is dated c. 5000, then we are left with a gap of 1500 years which is difficult to fill. It has not been possible to bridge the gap at Khirokitia, but at Troulli, on the northern coast *(Plate 9)*, an "intermediary" stage has been recognised and labelled Neolithic IB; this stage is associated with pottery, but it is not at all certain what the relation is between this pottery and that of the Neolithic II stage (the so-called Combed Ware). It may be earlier or later or contemporary. The gap of 1500 years thus remains a problem. The suggestion that during this period the island was abandoned as a result of a natural calamity and remained uninhabited does not seem very convincing[13]. It is incredible that Khirokitia, having remained abandoned from c. 5000 B.C., can have been rediscovered and reoccupied by new settlers c. 3500 B.C. Somewhere, one day, the missing links may be found. In the meantime, while the problem remains unsolved, it will be helpful and instructive to have more carbon 14 tests from Neolithic I and II sites, in order to test the accuracy of this method, at least as far as Cyprus Neolithic I and II are concerned.

The First Settlers

Apart from the chronological problem of the Neolithic period there is also the problem of the origin of the earliest settlers of Neolithic Cyprus. One may compare the Neolithic I period of Khirokitia, with its beehive houses, its stone vessels *(Plates 22, 31)*, and its custom of burying the dead under the floors of houses *(Plates 26, 27, 29)*, with similar phenomena in the Neolithic period at Jericho. But the Jericho pre-pottery stage (Neolithic A) is dated by carbon 14 to the early seventh millennium, whereas at Khirokitia no such early stage has yet been detected. A seventh millenium date has also been given to the Jarmo pre-pottery Neolithic culture in the upper Tigris valley, where stone vessels and flints have been found. But in spite of these similarities the Khirokitia Neolithic stands by itself.

Craniology has not been able to solve the problem of the origin of the early Neolithic settlers. One view is in favour of a distinct group not related to any neighbouring region. Another view suggests that the early settlers came from the Balkans (Thessaly-Macedonia) and another group from Cilicia[14]. All these, however, are apparently incompatible theories which are not yet substantiated by sufficient external evidence.

The Neolithic II period is marked by the arrival of a new culture, introduced by immigrants who established themselves mostly along the southern part of the island. The main settlements which have been excavated are at Kalavassos and Sotira. The new style in architecture, characterised by the semi-underground dwellings of Kalavassos, may be compared with those of the Beersheba culture in Palestine. This style, however, was soon abandoned, and free-standing houses of a more advanced type appear at Sotira *(Plate 28)*.

It is not certain to what extent Cyprus was connected commercially or otherwise with the cultures of other neighbouring countries. The presence on many Neolithic I sites (e.g. Khirokitia and Petra tou Limniti) of obsidian, which does not appear in the geological strata of Cyprus, suggests that some sort of relations existed between Cyprus and the south-eastern Anatolian coast. But the Neolithic culture which lasted 3500 years, one may strongly argue, was developed locally with little apparent influence from abroad.

Problems of the Chalcolithic and the Transition to the Early Bronze Age

About 3000 B.C. the Neolithic II sites come to an end, probably as a result of a natural disaster, and a new period begins, known as Chalcolithic I. The Chalcolithic settlements are more numerous than those of earlier periods; the best known is Erimi in the south of the island, excavated by Dikaios. There is a new and more exuberant style of pottery, the so-called Red-on-White ware *(Plate 25)*, in which abstract geometric and sometimes stylised floral motifs are depicted in orange paint on a white slip. There is more variety in the forms of clay and steatite statuettes, many of them representing a mothergoddess. A copper chisel makes its appearance for the first time in Cyprus at Erimi, justifying the name Chalcolithic given to this culture.

A new Chalcolithic I settlement has recently been discovered at Philia-Drakos[15], and has produced a regional variant of Red-on-White ware. Does this represent a cultural phase different from that of Erimi, or is it in fact a regional variation? Another problem which this new site presents is the presence of subterranean tunnels underneath the remains of houses hewn from the rock, used at the same time as the houses, but for an uncertain purpose.

Some have suggested a similarity between the new pottery styles of Erimi and those of Thessaly in the west and of Ras Shamra in the east. Nevertheless the Chalcolithic period is essentially a development from the Neolithic II stage in Cyprus, and cannot be said to have been seriously influenced by neighbouring countries.

The Chalcolithic I period ends c. 2500 B.C., and the Early Bronze Age period starts in 2300. There is yet another problem of filling a chronological gap between the two. Several efforts have been made, and a cultural stage known as Chalcolithic II has been discovered at Ambelikou, near the north-western coast, but the evidence is still too scanty. What is needed is the discovery of a site where continuous habitation can be traced from the Neolithic II period down to the Early Bronze Age.

The First Commercial and Cultural Contacts

The Early Bronze Age

The Early Bronze Age constitutes a distinct cultural phase, with innovations both in the material field and in burial customs. It is still a matter of controversy, however, which sites belong to the very beginning of this period. There are those who believe that there is an intermediate cultural stage, discovered in the region of Philia, distinguished mainly by the style of pottery *(Plates 35, 36, 44)*[16], but others reject this suggestion and regard the Philia culture as a regional phenomenon within the Early Bronze Age[17]. The pottery of the Philia culture, however, is important, because it is closely related to Anatolian pottery of the end of Early Bronze Age II. This period, dated to c. 2300 B.C., ended in a catastrophe in Anatolia. Since the beginning of the Early Bronze Age in Cyprus (Early Cypriote I) is also dated c. 2300, and considering the affinities already mentioned, the suggestion that the two phenomena should be related may seem justifiable[18]. New settlers may have come to Cyprus after the disaster which overtook the Anatolian sites. The fact that most of the sites belonging to the Philia cultural stage are situated round Morphou Bay may be indicative of the Anatolian origin of the first settlers; they gradually moved inland, and their pottery is found near Nicosia (Ayia Paraskevi).

The island was thickly populated in the Early Bronze Age period, and numerous settlements have been located, especially round the mining areas, for obvious reasons. Our knowledge of this period, however, comes almost exclusively from cemeteries, since no settlements have yet been excavated, and we have therefore no information about the architecture of this period. In the tomb offerings, however, there is a rich variety of objects which illustrate scenes from everyday life and even from religious life (clay models from Vounous, see below, p. 110). The simplicity of the Neolithic period is over. The wealth of the copper mines brings about an era of sophistication in the Bronze Age culture. There is evidence of commercial relations with the neighbouring Near Eastern countries; even with Minoan Crete there were some limited relations at the end of the Early Bronze Age. The few Minoan objects found on sites near the northern coast of Cyprus *(Plates 52, 53)* may have been brought directly by Cretans trading in copper from Cyprus, but this problem still awaits clarification. It will be interesting if it can be established that there were direct contacts between Cyprus and Crete as early as the end of the Early Bronze Age, since this will help to solve problems related to the borrowing from Crete of the first Cypriote syllabic script c. 1500 B.C.[19].

The Middle Bronze Age

The end of the Early Bronze Age in Cyprus marked an impulse of progress through commercial and cultural contact with neighbouring countries. This was the main pattern in the following period, the Middle Bronze Age, during which Cyprus took a prominent part in the affairs of the Near East. There was at the same time an atmosphere of preparation for an important change which took place at the end of the period, when

Cyprus entered the Late Bronze Age. Thus the Middle Bronze Age does not represent a distinct cultural phase but is in fact the epilogue to the Early Bronze Age and the prelude to the Late Bronze Age. The centre of importance shifts gradually from the north to the south and south-east of the island, near the coast, serving the trade with the harbour towns like Enkomi, the Tekké and Kition, which were to develop into large commercial centres during the Late Cypriote period.

It is not yet certain what were the causes of the changes, and the renewed intense contacts with the Syro-Palestine coast, towards the end of the Middle Bronze Age. It has been suggested that Cyprus may have been involved in the disturbances which afflicted the Near East during this period and that settlers from this troubled area established themselves in the eastern part of the island, trading from there with the Syro-Palestinian coast. There are some indications in support of this theory—for example the appearance of fortresses in various parts of the island—but the evidence is still insufficient to solve the problem. Other scholars believe that the disturbances for which there is evidence in Cyprus may have been due to internal Cypriote conflicts[20].

The Late Bronze Age

The new Cypriote cities traded freely with the Near Eastern countries, and Cypriote goods, especially pottery, were exported to the main Levantine centres. Copper, however, must have been the island's chief export. With the expulsion of the Hyksos from Egypt and the establishment of a *pax aegyptiaca* in the eastern Mediterranean, Cyprus offered an ideal centre for the development of trade relations between the Aegean and the East. The island was already known to the Cretans on their eastward journeys, but by c. 1400 B.C. the Mycenaeans dominated Knossos and replaced the Minoans in foreign trade. The wealth of Cyprus, mainly its copper *(Plate 60)*, and its ideal position for trade with the East soon

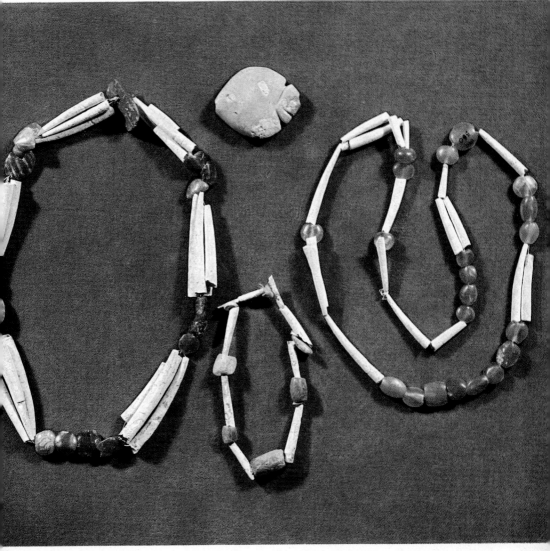

22, 23

30

31

32

attracted Mycenaean merchants. Mycenaean pottery is found in quantity in the tombs of Cyprus *(Plates 58–59, 70–73)*, especially in the cemeteries of the southern and eastern parts of the island. Was all this pottery imported, or was some of it made locally by Mycenaean craftsmen? This is a controversial problem which has not yet found its solution. A very high proportion of all known Mycenaean pottery comes from Cyprus. During the 14th and 13th centuries the tombs of Cyprus often contained as much Mycenaean as local pottery; sometimes, indeed, there were more Mycenaean than local vases. It seems likely that Mycenaean craftsmen established themselves in rich and cosmopolitan commercial centres like Enkomi, Kition and Kourion, and produced Mycenaean pottery, often imitating Cypriote and other Oriental forms *(Plate 58)*, but decorating them in a style which is Aegean. Even so, in the decoration of the large vases they exploited a repertoire of motifs known from other arts such as fresco painting or tapestry or ivory carving, and created a pictorial style in vase-painting, with representations of chariots, bulls, etc. *(Plates 70–73)*, which is peculiar to Cyprus, though a few examples are known from the Greek mainland and Rhodes. Clay analysis has not, in my view, solved the problem[21]. In other arts a similar phenomenon occurs. In glyptic art Aegean elements are found with Oriental motifs *(Plates 61, 62, 64)*. The same may be said of ivory carving *(Plate 92)* and jewellery *(Plates 86, 87)*. At a time of extensive commercial expansion, especially in the opulent world of the Orient, it would be natural to expect craftsmen to establish themselves quickly in the emporia of the East and produce works designed to please the exuberant taste of the Oriental princes and other wealthy patrons, at the same time borrowing styles and motifs from the artistic creations of the Orient. It is in this atmosphere that the Aegeo-Oriental art of the 14th and 13th centuries was created, the style which may also be considered as the first orientalising period of Greek art.

Some have suggested that Aegean colonies had been established in Cyprus as early as the 14th and 13th centuries. While I believe that Mycenaean traders and craftsmen established themselves during these periods in cosmopolitan centres like Enkomi and Kition, there is no evidence for such an early colonisation.

The problem of the Cypriote syllabic script is connected with the problems of the island's relations with the Aegean[22]. The first specimens of a syllabic script in Cyprus date from c. 1500 B.C. *(Plate 91)*, at a period when relations between Cyprus and the Aegean were not particularly close. If we admit that the earliest script was borrowed from Crete, since it has affinities with the Cretan Linear A script, we face the problem of how it was taken over by the Cypriots. Either we have to admit that relations between Cyprus and Crete existed at least as early as the 16th century, and that it is purely fortuitous that Cypriote objects of this period have not yet appeared on Cretan sites (or did the exports from Cyprus consist solely of copper?), or that the contact with the Cretans occurred on the Syrian coast, in Ugarit for example, where they both met as traders. This Cypro-Minoan script continued in use until the 12th century, though some rare specimens survive down to the 11th century in a language not yet known to us; the tablets from Enkomi, therefore, still remain undeciphered.

The efforts to read the text of the longest of these tablets as Greek have failed. This may be an additional argument suggesting that we cannot yet talk of Aegean colonisation before the end of the 13th century, at a time when an Eteocypriote and not a Greek language was in use in Cyprus.

Cyprus and Greece

The Achaean Colonisation

It was from the end of the 13th century onwards that Achaean settlers started coming to Cyprus; and by the end of the 12th century they had colonised and hellenised the island almost completely. This eastward movement of colonists coincides with the destruction of the mainland Mycenaean centres. A style of pottery known mainly from the Argolid and labelled Mycenaean III C: 1 is found in abundance on the floors of houses which were built soon after a destruction at the end of the 13th century *(Plate 96)*. At Kition and Enkomi this new pottery is almost the only type found, indicating the extent of the colonisation. Some scholars associate the destruction of the 13th century houses with an effort on the part of the Cypriots to repel the colonists[23], but this cannot be substantiated by archaeological evidence. The colonisation seems to have been a peaceful one, though, as might be expected, it caused a radical cultural change on the island. The fact that Mycenaean IIIC:1 pottery has been found on many sites on the island is indicative of its extent, though with a few exceptions these are mainly confined to the southern and eastern coasts.

A hitherto unsolved problem at Enkomi and other Late Cypriote towns in Cyprus is the location of the cemeteries associated with the first Achaean settlers. No tombs have yet been found containing Mycenaean IIIC:1 pottery. We know that the last burials just before the arrival of the Achaeans were in chamber tombs in the courtyards of the houses. In one case (Swedish excavations, Tomb 18) there is evidence for a burial which is almost contemporary with that event. Of the last occupants of the tomb one was provided with a large sword and the other with a pair of bronze greaves which were certainly imported from the Aegean. But no Mycenaean IIIC:1 pottery was found in the tomb. This means that to begin with some of the new settlers were buried in traditionally Cypriote tombs, but that later they buried their dead in a separate cemetery which, in spite of many efforts, has not yet been discovered.

A problem connected with Late Bronze Age Cyprus is that of the location of Alasia, which is mentioned in Oriental texts from the 18th down to the 11th century as a country which exported copper to the East[24]. It is commonly believed that this exporting country is Cyprus, but it is also often related to the Hittites, Syria and Egypt; some have even identified it with the city of Enkomi. The frequent references to Alasia in Hittite texts make the identification with Cyprus difficult, since there is no archaeological evidence of any relations between the two areas. The strongest argument in favour remains the fact that Alasia exported copper to these Near Eastern countries. If we accept that Alasia must be located in Cyprus, we have very little evidence to offer in favour of Enkomi as the site of Alasia. Kition has also produced evidence of copper-smelting, and probably other cities, not yet excavated, may do so also. Kition, as we know from the material discovered in tombs, had very close contacts with Egypt. Cyprus as a whole, therefore, and not any particular city on the island, may be considered as a candidate for identification with Alasia.

The End of the Bronze Age: Destruction and Resettlement

The *pax aegyptiaca* which permitted peaceful development, both commercial and cultural, on the island did not last until the end of the Bronze Age. The recent excavations at Enkomi, Sinda and Kition have produced abundant evidence that soon after the first Achaean colonisation these cities were destroyed by invaders, who have been identified with the Peoples of the Sea. After recovering from these invasions Cyprus received numbers of Levantine refugees, and towards the end of the 12th century a second wave of Achaean colonists established themselves on the island.

The Late Bronze Age cities of Cyprus were violently destroyed during the second quarter of the 11th century. At Kition the massive brick superstructure of the cyclopean city wall collapsed and fell on the street which ran parallel to it, and was never restored after the disaster *(Plates 56–57)*. The mud brick walls of houses collapsed, burying large jars and various implements on the floors of the houses.

The same phenomena appeared at Enkomi, and we may reasonably attribute this catastrophe to a severe earthquake. At Enkomi there is very scanty evidence for a short period of reoccupation after the catastrophe. The inhabitants had already started moving eastward to the coast, founding a new city, Salamis, round the natural harbour in the estuary of the river Pedieos. The silting up of the river harbour of Enkomi may have been another reason for the abandonment of this city. Recent excavations at Salamis by the Institut Courby of the University of Lyons under Professor J. Pouilloux have brought to light a tomb and remains which date from the beginning of the 11th century *(Plate 63)*. There must have been a period of about 25 years of coexistence before Enkomi was finally abandoned in favour of Salamis[25]. At Kition recent excavations show that even after the earthquake destruction there was a reoccupation throughout the city[26]. In several cases new houses were built on the ruins of those destroyed by the earthquake, and in other cases new thick floors were built in houses which had been repaired. Life continued into the 10th century, but the city was finally abandoned soon after 1000 B.C. The silting up of the Kition inner harbour may have been one of the causes.

It is within the framework of these events at the end of the Late Bronze Age that we have to interpret the legends relating to the foundation of cities in Cyprus by Greek heroes after the Trojan War[27]. The recent discoveries at Salamis which have been mentioned above present this problem in a new perspective. We need no longer say that Teucer and his comrades established themselves in the already existing city of Enkomi nearby. If we are to associate this colonial movement and the foundation of cities with the second wave of Achaean colonists who brought with them the Granary style of pottery, then we have to accept the foundation legend of Salamis as it is offered to us by tradition, namely that Salamis, the city which flourished in the 1st millennium, was the one founded by Teucer. Kition has no foundation legend, since the colonists inhabited the same site, building an early Iron Age city on the ruins of the old. The clue given

by the recent excavations at Salamis may serve as an incentive to re-exa
mine the problem of the foundation legends of the cities of Cyprus.

The late Professor J. Bérard, who carried out excavations in the region
of Paphos, tried to solve the problems connected with the foundation
legend which accepts Agapenor, king of Tegea, as the founder of this
town[28]. Agapenor was the leader of the Arcadians in the Trojan war, and
one would expect, if the legends were based on fact, to find in the region
of Paphos a city connected with the Achaean colonisation, i.e. a city with Mycenaean IIIC:1 pottery. Bérard tried unsuccessfully in the region of Ktima.
Kato Paphos (Nea Paphos) cannot be a candidate because the earliest
remains hitherto found there are no earlier than the 4th century. We know
that Kouklia (Palaepaphos) was an important Late Cypriote town, but
we also know of its king Kinyras who, according to the legends, was contemporary with Agapenor. The discovery by Dikaios at Palaeokastro-Maa
of a fortified Mycenaean town *(Plate 14)* associated with Mycenaean
IIIC:1 pottery may help to solve Bérard's problem, though this town had
admittedly a very short life and may have been used rather as an Achaean
stronghold like Sinda before the final domination by the Achaeans over
the whole island.

The Process of Cultural Hellenisation

The two centuries after the end of the Bronze Age are known as the Dark
Ages of Cypriote archaeology, as of Aegean archaeology. But whatever
happened during these two centuries, when Cyprus re-appears in the
scene of history it is already a Greek island, deeply affected by the Achaean
colonisation. Language, religion and culture in general are Greek. Tradi-
tions of almost five thousand years of connections with the East are over-
thrown, and within a period of less than two centuries the island turns
decisively to the West. This was of crucial importance to the later historical development of Cyprus.

The Cypriote syllabary continues to be employed, but is now used for the Greek language, as we can see from the first inscriptions of the 7th century, after the relative "illiteracy" of the Dark Ages. It remains, however, to explain the significant development of the script during the Dark Ages by finding inscriptions which will link the archaic script with that of the end of the Bronze Age.

How was the fusion of the Greek settlers and the autochthonous Cypriote element brought about? The true Cypriots (Eteocypriots) were in a majority, but gradually the Greek culture, being stronger and politically in an advantageous position, became dominant in the large cities, except at Amathus, where those of the Eteocypriots who resisted the new cultural influences gathered. We have evidence that as late as the 4th century B.C. the Eteocypriote language was spoken at Amathus. But in general the Greek culture did not extinguish the Cypriote culture. There was a harmonious fusion, though it was gradual and prolonged in some regions, and this is what distinguishes the Greek culture of Cyprus from that of the rest of the Greek world[29]. Gjerstad characterises this new culture in an epigrammatic phrase: "We hear the tunes of the new era forming the composition of a symphony with Mycenaean themes, Eteocyprian counterthemes, and Cypriote-Geometric combinations and development of both". This fusion was favoured also by the fact that Cyprus did not experience the cultural break caused in Greece by the Dorian invasion. This may be the cause of the conservative character of Cypriote culture, which may be observed throughout the Geometric and Archaic periods. In religion, burial customs, artistic tendencies and even language we observe clear survivals from the Mycenaean period, forming the true basis on which the Cypriote culture of the 1st millennium was built. It is this conservatism which helped the Cypriots to maintain the Greek character of their culture in spite of so many external influences introduced by the successive foreign dominations — Assyrian, Egyptian, Persian. This does not mean that the Oriental culture of the 1st millennium did not have any influence on Cypriote culture. There is always a mixture, the result of which was the creation of a lively archaic art in Cyprus *(Plates 98–112)*, greatly helped by the autonomy which the Cypriote kingdoms maintained in the city-state system even under Assyrian rule. Great wealth was also attained during the Archaic period, as is evidenced by the splendour of the royal tombs *(Plates 113, 114, 118, 142–143)* discovered during recent years.

In the Archaic period the Greek culture of Cyprus was strengthened by the arrival of Greeks who were on their way to the Levant to found colonies on such sites as Tarsus, Al Mina, etc. This renewal of contact made the Cypriots very conscious of their ethnic origins and their cultural heritage; this explains the historical events which followed in the classical period, when Cyprus joined forces with the rest of the Greeks in the long wars of independence against the Persians and in the cultivation of panhellenic ideals. This new spirit of Hellenism found its finest expression at the court of Salamis, which became the champion of Hellenic culture and led the wars of independence against the Persians.

There were Greek artists at the court of Salamis and elsewhere on the island; Cypriote artists, mainly sculptors, often created fine specimens of "Cypro-Greek" art, but the perfection of classical Greek art could not be attained by imitation. The unsettled conditions on the island and the preoccupation of the Cypriote kings with military matters did not favour the development of the arts. Cypriote art in general lost the originality it had shown in the archaic period and followed rather awkwardly the styles of Greek art. Cyprus thus entered the sphere of Greek culture as a mere province, and thereafter, and through the Hellenistic, Roman and Byzantine periods, the archaeology and history of the island had the same characteristics as the rest of the Greek world.

THE METHODS

II

The Organisation of Archaeological Work

The First Discoveries

Lack of method, as we have seen in the preceding chapter, caused considerable damage to Cypriote antiquities, especially during the second half of the 19th century. But even later, when the techniques of Cypriote archaeology had become more scholarly, the method of excavation was not always what we should consider today as really scientific. It may be said, however, that Cyprus utilised the new methods of scientific excavation earlier than other Near Eastern countries, and there was a time — and frequently this is still the case — when Near Eastern chronology depended to a considerable extent on that of Cyprus.

The organisation of the archaeological survey of Cyprus and the techniques of stratigraphy, recording and storage of finds which are described later in this chapter are in line with the practices current in modern archaeology, modified to suit local circumstances. Though professional archaeologists will be familiar with them they are presented here for the information of the general reader interested in this aspect of the subject.

The great majority of archaeologists working in Cyprus were interested mainly in the discovery of material as easily and quickly as possible. That is why until very recently we knew far more about tombs than about buildings. The abundant quantities of pottery and other objects usually found in the tombs of Cyprus of all periods attracted the archaeologists. The fact that there were generous laws regarding the division of finds was inevitably — and naturally — an extra incentive[30].

The Swedish Cyprus Expedition, having stayed on the island for more than three years (1927–1930) and excavated not only tombs but settlements and public buildings of all periods, developed proper stratigraphic methods which created a tradition in Cypriote archaeology. Of course they were not infallible. In the case of the Late Bronze Age site of Enkomi, having put their confidence in previous knowledge about the site (obtained in excavations by both villagers and archaeologists) they assumed that the site was only a necropolis and failed to observe that the necropolis was in reality integrated within the town, the tomb chambers being in the court-yards of the houses. It was left to Professor Schaeffer, leader of the French expedition (1934 onwards), to establish the true nature of this important site.

It was not only in the excavation of settlements, however, that errors were committed. In the excavation of tombs the dromoi were very often consi-dered as of no importance and remained unexcavated, or were sometimes excavated without proper care. The dromoi of the archaic royal tombs of Tamassos, excavated by Max Ohnefalsch-Richter in 1888, produced bronze horse trappings which the excavator misinterpreted as parts of armour[31]. It is only during the last few years, in the excavations by the Department of Antiquities of Cyprus in the necropolis of Salamis, that this phenomenon has been clarified. It was the custom in Cyprus in the 8th and 7th centuries B.C. to sacrifice horses in the dromoi of tombs in honour of the dead *(Plates 113–119)*. In several cases there were also chariots and fragments of furniture in the dromoi *(Plate 17)*. These were largely made of wood, which left its impression in the soil. It is only by careful excavation that this phenomenon has been observed and correctly identified *(Plate 19)*. In some ten tombs in the cemetery of Salamis skeletons of horses with all their bronze trappings *in situ* have been found, and in several cases the horses were associated with chariots. New and important information has thus been obtained, and indications from previous excavations can now be re-examined in the light of these discoveries. During the same period (1963) this phenomenon of horse sacrifice was observed in a tomb at Palae-paphos, which means that it may be looked for in other parts of the island as well as at Salamis. We may well wonder how many more such cases have been overlooked in the past. This new experience has contributed to improving the method of excavation of tombs, and similar methods are now used for stratification, etc., in excavating a cemetery. The results are rewarding, as will be seen below.

Written and Oral Sources

Literary and epigraphic information has also contributed to Cypriote archaeology. Among ancient authors only Strabo visited Cyprus, and his account may help to identify sites of later periods, especially in the Karpass peninsula. Hogarth in 1888 used Strabo extensively in identifying the sites mentioned by him[32], and during recent years Hogarth's identifications have been confirmed or corrected by the Archaeological Survey section of the Department of Antiquities.

Descriptions by travellers from the mediaeval period onwards are of importance to the modern scholar who is concerned with topographical problems. The descriptions and plans given by Mariti and Pococke of the city walls of Kition have been of considerable assistance to the present writer in the excavation of the city wall, which has now been rediscovered (in mediaeval times it was apparently standing well above the surface). Their descriptions are also of importance in the study of the ancient harbour of Kition, since the marshy area in which the harbour was originally situated has now been completely dried up by the systematic dumping of soil[33].

At Salamis the descriptions of earlier travellers help us to understand some of the monuments, even though they are not always accurate. The same may be said of the mediaeval maps of the site, and of the island in general, which do not often correspond to reality; their importance, however, is not negligible, as they often preserve place names which help in identifying sites. A 14th century traveller, Ludolf von Suchen from Westphalia (1336–1341), mentioned a monument in the necropolis of Salamis which is still known today as the Tomb or Prison of St Catherine. This monument has now been excavated, and it has been shown that it has been used continuously from the 7th century B.C. down to the present day, when it serves as a chapel *(Plate 114)*. The information given by this traveller has helped to clarify problems connected with the use of the building in the early Christian period; it is now clear that the tradition which survived from the 5th century A.D. down to the 14th century was not altogether fiction, though modern research has modified it in a number of respects[34].

We can also learn a good deal from descriptions by 19th century scholars. As a result of information provided by Salomon Reinach (reporting on the archaeological activities of M. Ohnefalsch-Richter in 1888) we have been able during the last few years to trace a hitherto unknown part of the necropolis of Salamis which has contributed considerably to our knowledge of burial customs during the Archaic and Classical periods[35].

Information from villagers is an important source, but it must always be scrutinised very carefully. In an old villager's mind a past discovery and everything which is connected with antiquities is always preserved very vividly, but is sometimes subject to considerable exaggeration when recounted to a present-day archaeologist. Bronze usually becomes gold; a terracotta statuette becomes a gold statue of Aphrodite. In the hands of a scholar who is familiar with the villager's mentality, however, such information may prove of value. A number of sites of settlements, cemeteries and sanctuaries have been identified during recent years on the basis of information supplied by villagers. In the Salamis area, where some of the most notorious tomb-robbers —whose fathers worked for Cesnola— are still living, we have had two characteristic instances of guidance from villagers during the last five years. Thanks to information from a tomb robber we re-excavated a tomb of the Archaic period which he had visited fifty years ago; in the chamber we found considerable quantities of pottery and an engraved silver bowl, and in the dromos a chariot and two horses with all their trappings. Certain negative information from tomb-robbers led to the excavation of the tumulus near Enkomi, which the British excavators reported in their publication to have been looted long ago. The excavation proved that the villagers were right, only there was no tomb but a cenotaph, with a rich pyre, missed by both tomb-robbers and archaeologists in the past[36].

At Kourion the late G. McFadden, acting on information from a villager, re-excavated the tomb where the famous gold sceptre of Kourion had been discovered by the tomb-robber himself, and by finding 11th century material in the tomb correctly dated the sceptre *(Plate 89)*[37]. This proved of considerable importance for dating the technique of enamel decoration on jewellery; for the absence of external archaeological evidence had led in the past to serious mistakes.

Place Names, Inscriptions and Surface Remains

Toponymics are always important, and may occasionally preserve the names of ancient cult places. An obvious example is the toponymic "Apollos" which is preserved in the area of the temple of Apollo at Kourion. But such toponymics should always be carefully scrutinised. In recent years a false toponymic was suggested to an archaeologist by the simple misplacing of a syllable: the correct toponymic "Asalayitos" used for the area of the "quiet stream" (without "salayi" = noiseless) which flowed past the site of Enkomi was given as "Alasayitos", and was thus erroneously, though in all good faith on the part of the scholar concerned, connected with the prehistoric Alasia of the cuneiform tablets of Anatolia and Tell el Amarna, as a survival of the ancient name and therefore as an additional justification for the theory suggesting the identification Enkomi-Alasia[38].

In other instances toponymics have actually been created on the basis of evidence produced by archaeology, e.g., the hill known as Kafizin, on which the cult place of a nymph was discovered in recent years. The hill is now also known as the "Nyfia".

There are various words in the modern Cypriote dialect which are used to denote ruins, remains of places inhabited in the past, castles or watch towers, sites littered with masonry rubble, sites with "tombs of the Greeks" (Ellinospilioi), which are more or less the same throughout the island. Many such toponymics have been examined by the Archaeological Survey Branch of the Department of Antiquities and have generally justified their names.

Epigraphic evidence for the identification of sites is rather meagre, though during the last few years it has been used with good results, mainly at Salamis. In the excavation of a large public building which was begun in 1952 by the Department of Antiquities many inscriptions were found mentioning the word gymnasium or naming a gymnasiarch. This helped to identify the building from the very beginning as a gymnasium, whereas previously it had been identified as a temple of Zeus or as a forum. The epigraphic evidence was several years later substantiated by the architectural plan which was gradually revealed, but it was possible from the very first year of the excavation to plan the excavation following the more or less standard plan of a gymnasium. Again at the same site inscriptions were found mentioning an amphitheatre which lay between the theatre and the gymnasium. A trial excavation between the two structures brought to light enough evidence to confirm the information given by the inscriptions.

Other public buildings, such as gymnasia, theatres, forums and baths, mainly of the Hellenistic and Roman periods, are mentioned in inscriptions found on the main city sites. These buildings have not yet been discovered, but the inscriptions may guide future excavators undertaking large-scale operations on such sites; they are also indicative of the importance of a site. The same may be said of temple sites such as that of Aphrodite Golgia at Golgoi, Artemis Paralia at Kition, Zeus Labranios at Phasoula (Limassol district) or Zeus Keraunios at Kition. In these instances the identification of the temple or sanctuary depended entirely on epigraphic evidence.

Surface surveys and surface discoveries have been of great assistance to modern archaeologists in identifying sites otherwise unrecorded and lying outside the limits of the city sites which are already fairly well known. This has been particularly the case with the discovery of Neolithic sites. It had already been established from the discoveries of the Swedish Cyprus Expedition that flints and axe-heads were quite common on Neolithic sites. The discovery of Khirokitia confirmed this, and also established another feature of a Neolithic site: the presence of a perennial spring nearby. These two features have helped to identify a considerable number of other sites, and we now have a fairly good picture of the extent of habitation in Cyprus during the Neolithic period.

Archaeological Mapping

A detailed survey of the whole island was envisaged when in 1955 the Department of Antiquities established a new branch of its services, the Archaeological Survey, with Dr H.W. Catling in charge. Its aim was to comb the whole of Cyprus and record on large-scale maps all the archaeological sites, known or unrecorded, from the Neolithic period down to mediaeval times. Index cards were prepared for all known archaeological sites (recorded in the files of the Department of Antiquities on the basis of visits by members of the staff from the establishment of the Department in 1935, and previously by members of the staff of the Cyprus Museum) together with references to reports, published or unpublished. New cards were prepared for all new sites discovered by the Archaeological Survey. These contain a brief description of the site, with map reference and a description of surface finds or special features. A thorough survey of the Kyrenia and Morphou districts has been completed, with results which are of the utmost importance for the study of the patterns of settlement during the various archaeological periods, especially during the prehistoric period[39]. The Archaeological Survey has its own headquarters, with sherd material from all sites which have been surveyed, photographic archives and maps. Apart from the purely scientific importance of the survey, a practical purpose is also served. From a large number of sites archaeologists can now choose the one most suitable for their investigations.

Chance discoveries during building or levelling operations are also recorded, and immediate rescue excavations are undertaken at places which are in danger of being built over or levelled. Such chance discoveries have greatly augmented the number of new sites, and some of them have contributed considerably to our knowledge of the archaeology of Cyprus. A striking example is the discovery of Late Bronze Age sherds in foundation trenches dug at Larnaca (the site of the ancient Kition) in 1959 for the building of a house. The evidence of these sherds took the chronology of the site of ancient Kition back to the Late Bronze Age, whereas previously it had been believed that Kition was a Phoenician foundation[40]. Systematic excavations undertaken by the Department of Antiquities since then have brought to light an important harbour town with imposing cyclopean defences dating from the Mycenaean period *(Plates 56, 57)*.

Techniques of Excavation

Stratigraphy

The stratigraphic method is used in all excavations by the Department of Antiquities and foreign expeditions. We shall describe the method which

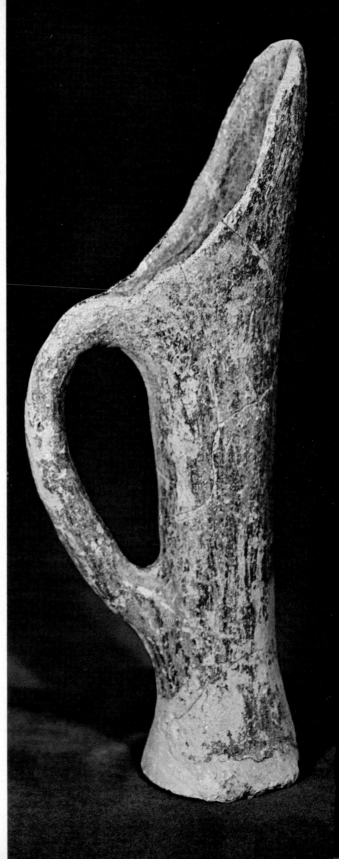

35, 36

37

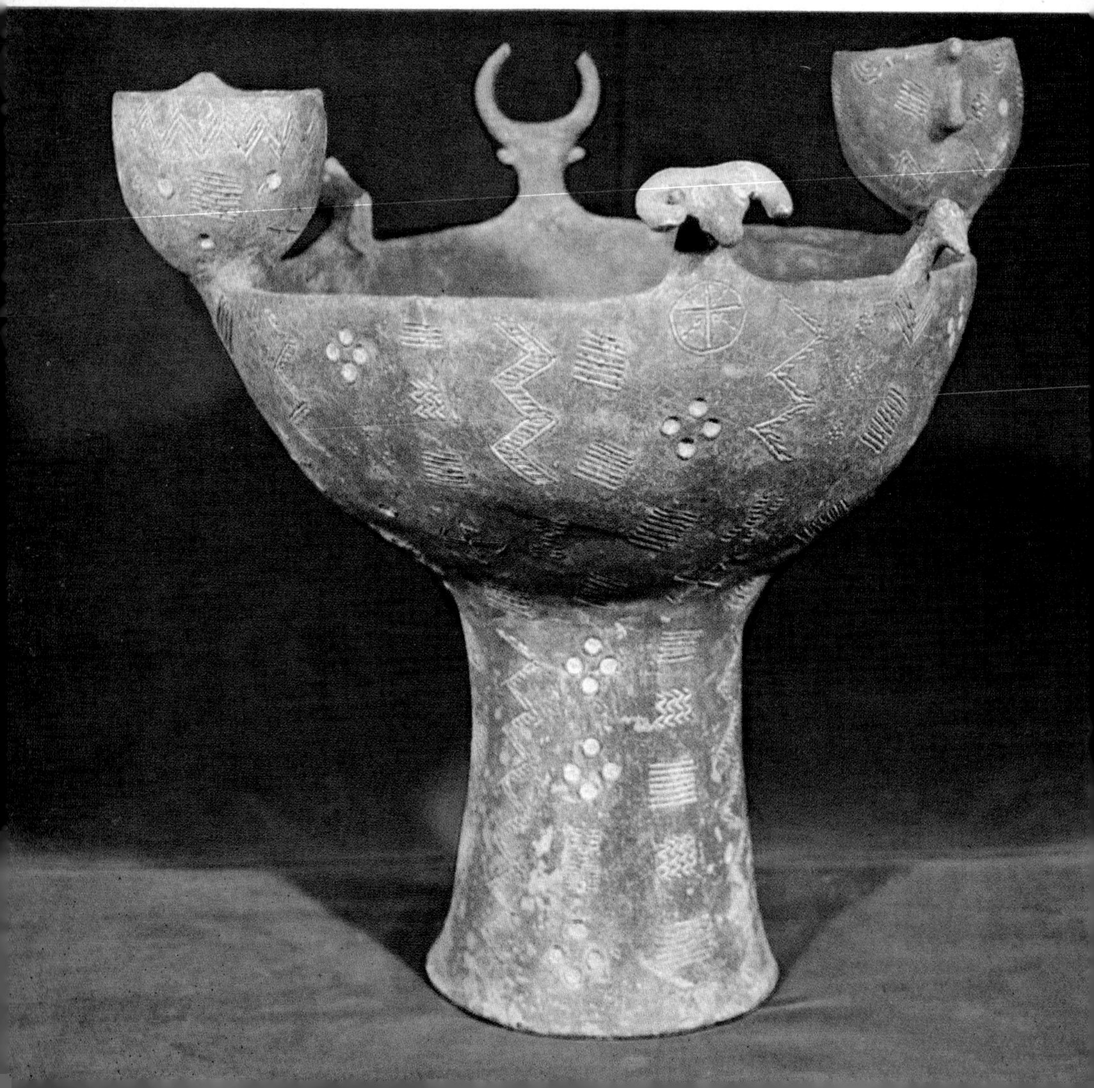

38, 39

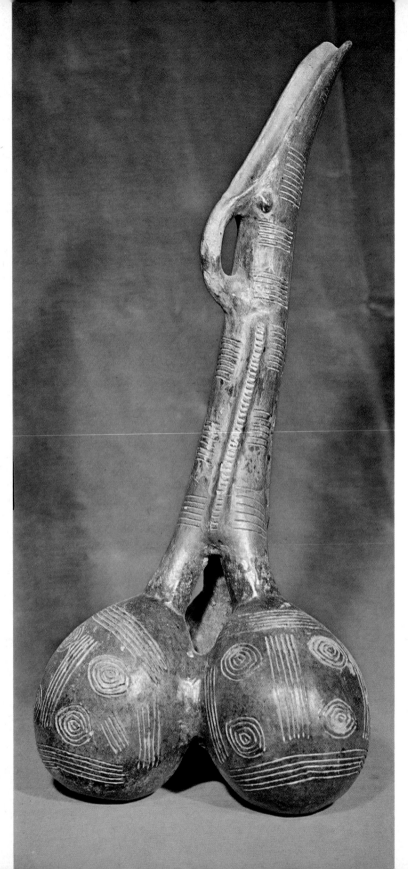

42, 43

44, 45

50, 51

52, 53

54, 55

is being used in the Department's current excavations at the Late Bronze Age city site of Kition.

The area of the excavation is divided into squares 3 m. by 3 m., baulks 50 cm. thick being left between the squares *(Plate 15)*. Sherd material is collected at depths of 15 cm., and in addition sherds of particular layers, however thin, are collected separately. When the floor of a particular room is found the room is allotted a number, and the sherds are now given the number of the room as well as the number of the square. Where necessary two separate cross sections, other than those of the squares, are left in a room to permit a fuller study of the succession of its floors *(Plate 18)*. The sherds are washed at the site, and the bags of sherds belonging to a particular square are grouped and described. A card is prepared describing the wares or objects found in each bag. Then, when the bags are brought to the Museum, separate cards are made from these field cards, describing the stratification of each particular room if there is one, or of a specifically defined small area. Sherds belonging to the same layer or the same floor are given an inventory number. The square is also indicated, and the position in relationship to a floor (above, below or embodied in flooring material) is given. The pottery is described on the card and the number of sherds of each ware is indicated. At the end a percentage for each layer is shown. Thus for each room and for each square we have a description of wares according to layers and floors from the surface down to bed-rock. Sherds bearing the same inventory number are put in the same wooden drawer, the various wares being separated by divisions. On the side of the drawer are written in large red letters the site, the inventory number, the number of the room, the square, the depth, and the floor or layer. All drawers containing material from one particular room are shelved separately. If among the sherds in one drawer there are any of particular importance these are given a sub-number, e.g., Inv. No. 135/1, 2, 3, etc. Effective control is thus possible and the study of the material by the archaeologist is greatly facilitated. This method, to the development of which Dr P. Dikaios made a considerable contribution, was also used in the earlier excavations by the Department of Antiquities at Enkomi.

Photographs and drawings of inventoried objects are of great importance. When the archaeologist goes through the material in the inventoried drawers he indicates which objects are to be photographed or drawn. This is done concurrently with the study of the sherds, so that the material may be ready for publication.

Clearance and Recording of the Site

Somewhat similar methods have been used in the excavation of tombs at Salamis. The stratigraphy in the filling of the large dromoi of the royal tombs can thus be carefully studied and the number of different burial periods ascertained. A longitudinal and a transverse cross-section are left in the dromos, and in both of these, especially the transverse section, one can see how the original filling of the dromos was disturbed for a second burial, when only part of it was removed in order to gain access to the *stomion* (mouth) of the chamber, and then replaced. This observation, together with the material found in the filling of each burial period, makes it possible to determine the date of each burial. Particular care is needed in cleaning the skeletons of the horses found on the floors of the dromoi. The bones are often so fragile that it is necessary to remove the soil from them either by pouring acetone on the hard accretions of soil and using a small sharp tool to remove them, or by gently blowing air on the bone through a cane. When a substantial part of the skeleton has been cleaned and has had time to dry off, it is impregnated with polyvinyl acetate, which hardens the bone and preserves the whole skeleton *in situ* for photographs and drawings *(Plates 115, 116)*. The bronze, iron or ivory trappings of the horses are cleaned in the same manner. Particular attention is paid to the excavation of chariots. It is easy to detect the metal portion, but the wooden pieces, which are the most substantial part, leave only their impression in the soil. Often these impressions are filled with soil softer than the rest, a dark or whitish stain (according to the nature of the wood) being left on the surface of the impression. By careful excavation and continuous observation it has been possible to determine the details of construction of the chariots which have been found, particularly in Tomb 79 (excavated in summer 1966) *(Plate 118)*. In the case of one of the chariots the impressions of the interlocked osiers of the chariot box showed up with sufficient clarity to be recorded in a photograph and a drawing[41].

Wooden furniture was also found in the dromos of Tomb 79. A whole throne of wood was found *(Plates 21, 134)*, all its parts being faced with thin narrow bands of ivory, plain or carved. The wood had disintegrated completely and only the ivory bands remained *in situ*. The ivory pieces were cleaned and strengthened with polyvinyl acetate. Pieces of thin cloth were fixed with polyvinyl acetate on each individual band of ivory and at the joints, so as to keep them together in their original position. Wire was fixed underneath the cloth along the main parts of the throne, and the whole object, having been freed of all the soil on which it rested, could be transferred for further treatment to the laboratories of the Cyprus Museum. Detailed drawings and photographs were prepared while the throne was *in situ*. In the laboratory each individual piece of the throne was given a number and was removed for treatment and repair (acetone being the only material used), and when all the pieces belonging to the throne had been treated in this manner they were fixed on a wooden frame as in the original throne *(Plate 134)*.

Skeletal remains found within the funerary chambers or in the dromoi are carefully preserved. In the case of human skeletons the skulls and the long members at least are preserved for the anthropologists, having been impregnated or brushed over with polyvinyl acetate to strengthen them. Such skeletal remains, especially skulls, are numbered and transferred to the Museum for study by craniologists and anthropologists. This study is of particular importance for the prehistoric periods, since it enables us to determine the ethnic and racial composition of a population[42].

The skeletons of horses are also important for determining the race of these animals in antiquity. The study of those found in the dromoi of 8th–7th century tombs at Salamis has revealed the existence in Cyprus during these periods of a horse which was much shorter than present-day breeds[43]. In some cases it was possible to distinguish the skeletons of asses from those of horses, the former always in association with less important tombs. When these skeletons are in good condition, they are left *in situ* under a glass cover, after having been studied and recorded in photographs and drawings.

Skeletons of smaller animals (chickens, fish) are removed for further treatment in the laboratory. They are strengthened with polyvinyl acetate; a thin cloth is applied to the whole surface, and in this manner the whole skeleton can be undercut, detached from the soil and removed safely to the laboratory, without any disturbance of the individual bones, for cleaning and study.

Scientific Investigations

Chemical analysis of organic or inorganic objects and substances plays an important part in field archaeology. The bottoms of large amphorae may contain a solid spongy substance mixed with soil, which if analysed may show what the amphora contained—e.g., honey, oil or wine.

At the Cellarka site in the necropolis of Salamis careful excavation, with squares and sections over the whole area, produced some unexpected phenomena. Among the tombs, on the bed-rock surface and outside the fillings of the dromoi, a number of pyres were found, obviously associated with the dead *(Plate 149)*. Offerings of small clay vases and figurines *(Plate 137)* but mostly of carbonised fruit—almonds, figs, grapes, etc. *(Plate 152)*—were also found. The normal method of excavating tombs would have missed this important funerary custom. A necropolis, however, must be considered as a whole, not merely as a collection of separate tombs. The carbonised fruits have been collected and have already been analysed by Dr Helmqvist in Stockholm. Pieces of unburnt wood from posts have been found in holes on the terrace of the 4th century B.C. cenotaph of King Nicocreon in the Salamis necropolis *(Plate 155)*. These, together with pieces of wood from present-day trees, have been sent for analysis. In modern archaeology, therefore, science is at the disposal of the field archaeologist; but at the same time archaeology provides science with invaluable opportunities for specific studies such as those mentioned above.

Apart from the carbon 14 method which is now used extensively for the dating of prehistoric sites, and which has been successfully applied in dating the main Neolithic settlements of Cyprus, other scientific methods have also been employed. Archaeomagnetism has been used at Enkomi in Professor Schaeffer's excavations, with Dr Aitken in charge, to detect the road system of the city, with satisfactory results. Air photography has not yet been used extensively for the detection of new archaeological sites, but there is a complete coverage of air photographs for Cyprus which is often consulted for the better understanding of the physiognomy of known archaeological areas. It may be mentioned that an air photograph disclosed the lost continuation of the Roman water conduit near the Kourion stadium when the investigator despaired of finding it. It showed a darker line of slightly denser vegetation growing in a rock-cut trench.

A method which has been used with Cypriote material, though not in Cyprus, is the analysis of clay from Mycenaean sherds found in Cyprus and at sites on the Greek mainland in order to determine the origin of the so-called Cypro-Mycenaean vases. These experiments have been carried out at Oxford under the guidance of Dr Catling, who also published the archaeological report. This is not the first time that this method has been employed: in the United States in particular it has been used extensively. In 1961 Dr Philip Hammond pointed out the shortcomings of this method in resolving problems such as the origin of vases by means of spectographic analysis, and I believe that his remarks are still valid to-day: "The very nature of pottery is such, chemically, that it is highly dangerous to attempt to generalise upon it. Significant variants may well occur between widely separated clay pits but, and more importantly, significant variations may also occur within layers and areas of *one* pit, as well as from factors associated with handling, tempering and firing"[44].

The analysis carried out at Oxford indicated that all Mycenaean vases from Cyprus were imported from the Greek mainland[45]. There are, however, various archaeological arguments against accepting the absolute terms of this verdict, and it would, I believe, be premature to surrender to a method which it is "dangerous to attempt to generalise upon".

Cleaning, Restoration and Preservation

The Workshop and the Laboratory

A properly conducted excavation is not complete without an efficient laboratory and workshop which will take over the material from the field and make it ready for study and exhibition in a museum showcase. It has often been during this transitional period that many valuable objects of metal or faience or ivory have disappeared or disintegrated for lack of proper scientific treatment. It is not surprising that in old reports on excavations metal objects are seldom mentioned, the reason being that they did not survive the trip from the field to the museum or fell into powder after rapid corrosion in a damp museum store-room. The Cyprus Museum is equipped with a modest laboratory where almost all cases can be dealt with. Metal objects, if containing sufficient metal in them, undergo treatment by the electrolysis method—unless the patina of an object must be conserved, in which case other methods are employed. If there is no metal at all in an object and nothing but corrosion is left, it will have to undergo treatment in successive chemical solutions until all traces of active corrosion disappear. This, however, is a long process, and in a country like Cyprus where there are several excavations going on concurrently each year, a small laboratory cannot have sufficient resources to meet all demands. New techniques have been announced enabling a large number of metal objects to be put in the same tank; and thanks to an automatic changing of the chemical solutions and automatic checking of chlorides the process is expedited and much space is saved[46].

Though examination by X-rays has not yet been employed in Cyprus, nevertheless it has been applied to objects from excavations in Cyprus, for instance to the silver bowl from a 14th century tomb excavated by Professor Schaeffer at Enkomi *(Plate 75)*[47]. The bowl was in direct contact with bronze objects in the tomb and its surface had acquired the green corrosion of the bronzes. It was sent to Dr Plenderleith, at that time head of the British Museum laboratory, who with the help of X-rays saw that underneath the green corrosion there was silver, and on the silver body of the vase there was an inlaid decoration of gold and niello. This determined the process of treatment, and thus the valuable bowl was saved. The X-ray method is now extensively used in photographing decorated bronze bowls in the British Museum; by this process any decoration or inscriptions under the corroded surface of a metal object appear clearly on the X-ray photograph before treatment.

The Modern Museum

In the arrangement of objects in the Cyprus Museum Dr P. Dikaios, Curator of the Museum for nearly thirty years, has followed the "didactic" method[48]. Objects from the Neolithic and Early Bronze Age periods are grouped separately. There follows a large collection of pottery, sculpture, bronzes and jewellery from the early periods down to Roman times, arranged chronologically. A special feature is the gallery of reconstructed tombs, where one may follow the development of tomb architecture and burial customs from the Neolithic down to the classical period.

New galleries have now been added to the Museum: one for inscriptions, where the development of the Cypriote script from the 16th century B.C. (the Enkomi tablets) down to the Early Christian period can be studied. There is also a gallery of funerary reliefs, and a large exhibition gallery is to be devoted to the main Late Bronze Age excavations of recent years at Enkomi, Kition and Kouklia.

The objects on show represent only a small fraction of the antiquities in the Cyprus Museum. Large reserve collections are suitably stored in the "Students' Galleries", which are accessible to scholars for study. The objects are arranged typologically and chronologically.

In a country where excavations are carried out every year the problem of space is always acute. District museums have been established in the main towns, as well as site museums at the main archaeological sites, which supplement a visit to the architectural remains.

Preservation of Sites and Structures

The Department of Antiquities of Cyprus with its Monuments Branch is wholly responsible for the conservation of archaeological sites and ancient monuments. Of the archaeological sites the most difficult to maintain are those of the prehistoric period, where the walls are built of rubble and mud. Instead of covering them with a roof, which would be both expensive and aesthetically objectionable, we find that strengthening the surface of the walls with mud-coloured cement concrete is a satisfactory method: in the first place it conserves the character of the wall unaltered, since the original stones are replaced in their original positions, and secondly the concrete which replaces the mud can resist any weather conditions. The Neolithic remains of Khirokitia, excavated some thirty years ago, are by this means preserved in very good condition. The same method is now being applied to the extensive Late Bronze Age remains of Enkomi, where, apart from a few ashlar block buildings, the great bulk of the walls are built of rubble and mud. The same method has been applied to the remains of the palace of Vouni (classical period) excavated in 1930, and to the remains of the Roman period at Kourion.

The large public buildings recently discovered at Salamis, built with large ashlar blocks, present different problems. The walls of these buildings, mainly those of the Gymnasium, which were preserved to their original height, had lost their verticality in several instances as a result of pressure or because the deep roots of the forest trees which grew above them had penetrated the joints and dislocated the blocks of stone. Such walls had to be pulled down and rebuilt after careful drawings and detailed photographs had been obtained of their original position. Wall mosaics and frescoes were found in the niches of the gymnasium baths *(Plates 173, 175, 176)*. These have been left *in situ*, but they were treated with chemicals so as to protect their surface from the saline atmosphere or the sea. Often large parts had to be removed and reset so as to make the back of the mosaic or fresco moisture-proof.

Inscribed marble slabs found built into later walls or floors have been replaced by replicas in white cement. Statues of marble have been taken to the Famagusta District Museum and the Cyprus Museum in Nicosia, but some of the headless statues which were considered as of secondary importance were left *in situ*, round one of the swimming pools in the gymnasium, thus making a kind of open-air museum of sculpture. The white or grey marble standing out against the yellow sandstone walls, with mimosas in the background, is of very pleasing effect *(Plate 174)*.

It was more difficult to preserve and present as ancient monuments the large royal tombs of Salamis. The long dromoi, after we had taken away the large jars and other objects, would not present any interest for the visitor. We have, however, left the skeletons of the horses *in situ*, and in one case the impressions left by the wooden parts of the chariot, the pole and the yoke. The whole structure has been impregnated with polyvinyl acetate; the edge has been strengthened with cement of the same colour as the soil, and a glass and metal shelter has been provided.

A long-term preoccupation, however, of the Monuments Branch of the Department, with its trained masons and technicians, is the preservation and restoration of the Byzantine and mediaeval monuments which are to be found all over the island.

Principles of Chronological Classification

The study of Cypriote archaeology, like that of Cretan archaeology, has its own problems and methods, and there are scholars who specialise in this study. One of the main problems to be faced is the chronology of the various periods, which is based on the dating of the various classes and types of objects. This is particularly the case with the early periods, where the evidence of coins and inscriptions, which might have given an absolute dating, is lacking.

The carbon 14 method has been used for the Neolithic and Chalcolithic periods, with good results[49]. For the Bronze Age the chronology is based mainly on imports from Syria (for the Early Bronze Age) and from Crete (for the Middle Bronze Age) or on Cypriote objects found on Near Eastern sites or in Crete.

For the Late Bronze Age we have the evidence of the Mycenaean pottery, the stylistic development of which can be followed fairly closely. The Mycenaean sherds found at Tell el Amarna (destroyed in 1375 B.C.) give a more or less absolute date to a stylistic group of which it is easy to follow the development. Imports from the Aegean continue right through from the early Geometric to the classical periods, and Cypriote objects are found on many Near Eastern and Greek sites. The chronology of the first millennium has been established with good synchronisms by Gjerstad in his monumental work *The Swedish Cyprus Expedition* IV (2). One period, however, on which there is now disagreement is Cypro-Archaic I, dated by Gjerstad to c. 700–600 B.C. Various arguments for a higher date have been put forward. Recently a Euboean bowl has been found in a tomb at Palaepaphos which also produced pottery of the Cypro-Archaic I period. At Eretria, in Euboea, several fragments of Cypro-Archaic I pottery have been found associated with fragments of bowls of the same type as that from Palaepaphos. These bowls are dated to the second half of the 8th century. This synchronism may make the higher date for Cypro-Archaic I a necessity[50].

From the end of the 6th century B.C. onwards we have numismatic and epigraphic evidence, as well as the firmly dated Attic pottery which is found in abundance along with other Greek products. Literary evidence also makes its contribution. Information furnished by late Greek authors about the death of Nicocreon, the last king of Salamis, who committed suicide along with other members of the royal family, helped to identify his cenotaph in the necropolis of Salamis.

Underwater Archaeology and the Study of Ports

In discussing archaeological research we normally think of research on land. During recent years, however, a new branch of archaeology has developed—subaqua or underwater archaeology, which deals with remains of ancient civilisations, whether shipwrecks or submerged settlements, on the sea-bed.

Underwater research has many possibilities in Cyprus, especially now that its methods have been perfected to enable archaeologist-divers to apply orthodox techniques of "excavation" and carry out adequate surveying and recording at the bottom of the sea. On many occasions amateur divers have recovered vases and terracotta figures from the sea-bed, particularly in the bay of Salamis, but no systematic survey has yet been undertaken.

Salamis and Nea Paphos

Harbour towns like Salamis, Amathus and Paphos deserve large-scale investigation, not only in the hope of discovering shipwrecks, which must be numerous, but also for the study of their harbours. The harbour of Salamis, which must have been one of the most important in the Near East, offers excellent opportunities. Architectural remains of harbour works are still visible on the sea-bed, very near the shore, and at high tide they appear on the surface. The outer part of the harbour is still navigable by small boats, but naturally the bay itself is shallow as a result of the long process of silting up which had already started in antiquity. The artificial breakwaters running from north to south extend northward to connect with a reef, partly natural and partly artificial, which protected the seaward side of the city. At a point about two miles north of the main harbour this same reef serves as breakwater to another auxiliary harbour of late Roman date. We know, however, that Demetrius Poliorcetes made use in 360 B.C. of a second harbour to the north of Salamis, and this may be the one. It was traced some ten years ago by amateur divers.

The harbour of Nea Paphos *(Plate 167)* must have been of importance for the trade with the Aegean, especially in Hellenistic and Roman times when this city was the capital of the island. Amateur divers brought a number of Roman marble statues from the bottom of the sea in 1958; and during deepening of the present harbour area in 1965 literally thousands of stamped amphora handles were brought to light.

The harbour was mainly artificial, with two long breakwaters, one of which survives to a length of 350 m. and the other to a length of 170 m. They formed an extension of the city wall, and were constructed of large blocks of stone joined with metal cramps. The harbour is still partly used, but its eastern part has been silted up and is now marshland. It was also used in mediaeval times, when two fortresses were built on its western arm; one of these still survives.

Enkomi and Kition

The quest for the Late Bronze Age harbours of Enkomi and Kition will certainly prove difficult. Both these harbour towns, at a distance of one or two kilometres from the sea, were originally connected with it by a navigable channel. The area in between was marshy land which is still traceable. The marshes of the harbour of Kition were filled with soil only forty years ago, while those of Enkomi are still noticeable during the rainy season. It would be of great interest to discover the former navigable channels. It may be that the excavations at Kition will one day throw light on its harbour, since the area of the city wall where investigations are now going on is very near the harbour itself. The rectangular bastions of the city wall must have had the marshes coming right up to their base, as is the case now, after the excavations—the water level being about a metre above the foundations. The large number of stone anchors found near the city wall—used as building material in constructions of the 12th century B.C.—may indicate that the harbour itself is somewhere in the vicinity.

Soloi

Soloi provides another example of the silting up of an ancient Cypriote harbour; the entire harbour area has been overlaid with detritus to a depth of about a metre above the present water table. Trial pits dug here in 1958 disclosed traces of walls and buildings associated with the port and its defences. The evidence points to a principal occupation period from the 4th century B.C. to the 2nd century A.D. Among other ancient ports which also appear to have been silted up in this way are Dhekelia and Amathus (where the remains of a massive masonry construction can be seen on the foreshore) *(Plate 1)*.

THE RESULTS

III

New Light on a Dark Age

The Neolithic Civilisation of Khirokitia

The most important of the Neolithic settlements is undoubtedly Khirokitia, excavated by P. Dikaios for the Cyprus Department of Antiquities
during the years 1936–1939 and 1946[51]. Khirokitia is built on a small hill
at the foot of which flows the Maroniou river, which contains water only
during the rainy season *(Plates 11, 12)*. There are perennial springs not
far from the settlement. South of the settlement is fertile land which the
Neolithic settlers must have cultivated. Agriculture must have been one
of their main occupations: stone querns and sickle-blades of flint have
been found in abundance on the floors of houses. Hunting of wild animals,
such as stags, wild goats and mouflons, must also have been practised, as
is indicated by the presence of flint arrowheads. At the same time, however, the settlers had started domesticating animals such as pigs, goats and
sheep.

Only part of the settlement has been excavated (about fifty dwellings), but
originally the whole of the habitable surface of the hill must have been
occupied by houses. The houses consist of a circular room *(tholos)* resembling a beehive. They vary in size, the largest having a diameter of 10 m.,
and the walls are fairly thick (up to 3 m.). The lower part of the tholos is
constructed of rubble masonry set in mud, and upon this rests a dome of
sun-dried mud bricks or pisé. There must have been an opening at the top
as an outlet for the smoke from the central hearth. The largest of the Khirokitia huts had a kind of platform of wooden beams and brushwood
supported on two masonry pillars.

Though each house usually consisted of a single tholos, there are a few
cases belonging to a developed stage of the Khirokitia culture in which

the main tholos is accompanied by two subsidiary ones, used as a kitchen and workshop respectively, all standing in a courtyard enclosed by a boundary wall. The tholos shows considerable skill in architecture, and may be compared with other developed pre-pottery Neolithic cultures of the Near East, especially Jericho. There was no attempt, however, at a particular arrangement of the tholoi, which were huddled closely together on either side of a street paved with limestone and andesite river pebbles. The street crossed the settlement obliquely from the south bend of the river up to the top of the hill. There is evidence that it also crossed the northern side of the hill, which must also have been inhabited, and led down to the river again. This must have been the main street of the settlement, and therefore of great importance for access to the water supply and other needs of the community; it was repeatedly repaired and added to as the floor levels of the houses rose throughout the long life of the settlement. After the excavations, which have reached right down to its foundations, it looks like a defensive wall rather than a street.

The tholoi, with hearths, benches and tools on their floors, were used for habitation. But in pits in the floors of the houses the inhabitants of Khirokitia also buried their dead in a contracted position, with the knees bent against the chest *(Plates 26, 27, 29)*. Gifts were offered to the dead, mainly stone bowls which were broken ceremonially as part of the funeral rites. With the skeletons of women necklaces of cornelian and dentalium beads were also found *(Plate 23)*. Occasionally—so great was the fear of the dead—heavy stones were placed over the bodies to ensure that they would remain still. This may have also been the reason for burying the dead within the house, so as to appease their souls which might otherwise have harmed the living.

There was a high mortality among infants under one year old. In a single tholos twenty-five infants were found.

Though agriculture and hunting were the main occupations of the Khirokitians, they also found time for other activities indoors. They made vessels of andesite which they collected from the nearby bed of the river; the main form was a bowl, shallow or deep, with or without spout and handle *(Plates 22, 31)*. By rubbing one stone into the other they succeeded in producing perfect shapes, with thin walls, sometimes decorated with relief or engraved decoration. There must also have been vessels of other perishable materials such as wood and leather. Tools were made of andesite or flint and bone. The obsidian implements constitute a refinement which must have been imported, since obsidian does not exist in the geological strata of the island; possible sources may have been Anatolia or Northern Syria. Spindle whorls and needles suggest that the Khirokitians wove textiles: clearly they had attained an advanced stage of culture.

Khirokitia has also produced the earliest specimens of sculpture: small figures of andesite, without any indication of sex, with violin-shaped bodies and with simple indications of facial characteristics *(Plate 34)*. They show a striking resemblance to the well-known marble idols from the Cyclades, but this may be accidental. A unique head of unbaked clay, probably that of a woman, shows an effort to render the facial characteristics more realistically *(Plate 30)*.

We have discussed the Neolithic culture of Khirokitia in some detail, since it is the earliest culture of the island and, as such, already shows the characteristics of an organised community of food-producing farmers who, as we can see from the archaeological discoveries, also had certain religious and artistic preoccupations.

As already noted in the chapter on Problems, we have to account for a gap of about 1500 years before we reach the second phase of the Khirokitia culture. This stage is also represented on a number of other sites, the most important of which—Kalavassos and Sotira—have been excavated by P. Dikaios for the Cyprus Department of Antiquities[52] and the Pennsylvania University Museum respectively[53]. This new culture is chiefly characterised by the introduction of pottery, the so-called Combed Ware *(Plate 24)*, by new settlers who may have come from somewhere in Palestine. These settlers also introduced new types of houses. At Kalavassos these consisted of circular pits hewn from the bed-rock, with traces of a light roof of wattle and daub supported on a central post. At Sotira a considerable area of the Neolithic settlement was excavated on the level top of a hill *(Plate 28)*. The houses at Sotira present a great variety of ground plan, in contrast to the uniformity of the houses of the early phase at Khirokitia: they range from the circular type to an oval or rectangular plan with rounded corners.

The main difference between the Sotira culture (Neolithic II) and the early Khirokitia culture (Neolithic I) is that at Sotira the dead were buried in a nearby separate cemetery. The Combed Ware which is found on all sites of the Neolithic II period must have reached a developed stage in its place of origin before it was introduced to Cyprus. Large jugs and spouted bowls are the commonest types. The surface of the vases has a dark brown semiglossy slip which was "combed" with an instrument while the paint was still wet, producing multiple wavy bands which give the vase an exceptionally attractive appearance with the interplay of dark and light brown colours.

The Neolithic culture of Cyprus, extending over a period of more than 3500 years, marks the earliest appearance of the island on the scene of Mediterranean culture. It is a bold and impressive achievement, comparable in greatness with that of other Near Eastern countries, which gives expression to the personality and character of Cypriote culture throughout this long period.

Erimi and its Red-on-White Ware

This period, represented by the culture of Erimi (a site 8 miles west of Limassol excavated by Dikaios for the Cyprus Museum, 1933–1935)[54], prepared Cyprus for its exuberant entrance into the Bronze Age. A rich material culture developed on the already thickly populated island. New forms appear in pottery, with a rich variety of painted decoration (Red-on-White). The motifs, linear or floral, show an extraordinary imaginative force *(Plate 25)*.

In some ways they are the forerunners of another great period in Cypriote vase-painting, the Archaic period. The floral motifs, though stylised, show considerable freedom, but also a marked skill on the part of the painter in applying them with meticulous care on the ample white surface of the vase.

The minute details of the geometric patterns in composite arrangements recall the perfection attained in much later periods. The Cypriote crafts-man invented new forms in sculpture, using a new material: steatite. The mothergoddess now makes her appearance in the cross-shaped stylised figurines of steatite *(Plates 32, 33)*, resembling in many ways the Early Cycladic idols. They show undoubted artistic merit, judged even by modern standards, with something of the style of Modigliani. In clay, where more freedom and realism are shown, the breasts and genitalia are particularly emphasised. There are also double figurines in steatite, one male and one female, their bodies disposed in the form of a cross. Some of these have been found recently in newly discovered Chalcolithic sites in the Paphos district, where a stone sculpture industry seems to have been particularly well developed[55].

A copper chisel found at Erimi provides justification for the Chalcolithic designation given to this period. It was a period in which wide cultural horizons had already been created. The new product, copper, was destined to broaden these horizons beyond the shores of the island, free Cyprus from its Neolithic isolation, and place it on the map of the Near East as an important country which was in a position to exchange influences with its neighbours.

The Early Bronze Age Culture of Philia

Though the island was thickly populated during the Early Bronze Age, its culture is insufficiently known, for none of the numerous settlements has yet been excavated. What we know about it is based almost exclusively on the evidence from tombs. Only one house at Alambra and scattered remains at Ambelikou offer slender information about the architecture of this period[56]. The house at Alambra was L-shaped consisting of two adjoining rooms, rectangular in plan, with courtyards in front of them, surrounded by a wall on the west and south sides. The lower parts of the walls were built of stone, the upper of sun-dried mud bricks; the house may have had a flat roof. The houses at Ambelikou had rooms which were also rectangular in plan.

The cemeteries are now definitely outside the settlement area, usually on the slope of a hill. During the early part of this period, known as the phase of the Philia culture (see Chapter I), the tombs are either oval pits, hewn from the rock, or natural caves along the edge of a plateau. Numerous offerings are found in these tombs, mainly pottery and bronzes which testify to the sudden influx into the island of a new culture related to that of Western Anatolia. We have already noted in Chapter I that this may have been due to the arrival in Cyprus of new settlers from Western Anatolia, after the disaster which befell that area in Anatolian Early Bronze Age 2 (which is contemporary with the very beginning of Early Cypriote I). Thus side by side with some traditional Cypriote forms of Red Polished and Red-on-White ware we encounter others which are distinctly Anatolian such as the jug with a broad flat base, tall neck and beaked spout *(Plates 35, 36)* and a new type of pottery, the Black Slip Combed Ware which may have originated in S.E. Anatolia.

This stage of culture is confined mainly to the area round Morphou Bay, but it also penetrated as far as Ayia Paraskevi (Nicosia) and Vasilia (Kyrenia district) and, on the south coast, to Anoyira and Sotira. P. Dikaios, who investigated a number of tombs at Philia itself (1943, for the Cyprus Department of Antiquities) believes that the close Anatolian connections of this culture put it at the very beginning of the Early Bronze Age, at the time when the foreign elements were introduced directly from Western Anatolia and had not yet been adopted by the local culture. J.R. Stewart, who excavated at Vasilia and Ayia Paraskevi in 1955, believed that the Philia culture was a regional phenomenon within the Early Bronze Age, but in view of its wide distribution from the north to the south coast such an interpretation is no longer possible[57]. Whatever interpretation one may accept, it cannot be denied that this culture stands by itself, bearing witness to the earliest contact with Western Anatolia. It is not by any means primitive: side by side with the pit tombs of Ayia Paraskevi we find the majestic chamber tombs of Vasilia, with their rich bronzes (a fine dagger and three heavy bronze armlets) and alabaster vases, a jug and a large bowl, 58 cm. in diameter, evidently imported from Egypt.

The Necropolis of Vounous

The development of the Early Bronze Age culture may be followed at the vast necropolis at Vounous, which was excavated by P. Dikaios for the Cyprus Museum (1931–32) and by J.R. Stewart for the British School at Athens (1937). At first we notice the adaptation of Anatolian elements in pottery to suit the taste of the Cypriote potter, but later the Cypriote elements become predominant. The numerous rock-cut chamber tombs of Vounous have yielded a large variety of vases.

Their lustrous surface is often decorated with engraved patterns and ornaments in relief, and even with plastically rendered figures *(Plates 37–39)*. The flat-based Anatolian jugs gradually fade out, and older Chalcolithic shapes with pointed and rounded bases reappear: the Cypriote tradition is once more triumphant. The exuberance of the Cypriote potter during the last phase of the Early Bronze Age passes imagination. Large composite vases *(Plates 40, 41)*, richly decorated with engraved patterns, spouted bowls decorated with birds, bucrania or human and animal figures in the round, depicted in scenes from daily life, are common themes in the potter's repertoire. This exuberance is no doubt a reflection of the material prosperity of the island resulting from the export of copper. Apart from pottery the tombs of this period have also yielded jewellery in gold *(Plate 50)* and silver (hair ornaments) and necklaces of faience and stone beads, as well as numerous weapons and tools of bronze. There are also plank-shaped idols with incised decoration *(Plate 51)*, and plastic vases in the form of animals *(Plate 48)*, which show both artistic ability and a sense of humour, two qualities which the Cypriote coroplast never lacked. The most remarkable objects, however, are two compositions in clay, representing a sanctuary *(Plate 49)* and a ploughing scene *(Plate 47)* respectively, both found in tombs at Vounous (Cyprus Museum excavations). They deserve a detailed description.

The first of these objects represents a *temenos* where a ritual ceremony is taking place. It has the shape of a circular enclosure, within which are those participating in the ceremony. Attention is centred upon three human figures in relief on the wall opposite the entrance. They seem to be wearing bulls' masks and holding snakes in their hands. In front of them is a kneeling figure, and another crowned figure is seated on a throne. There are other figures seated on benches on either side of the masked figures, and others standing in groups. On either side of the entrance are bulls in pens awaiting sacrifice, attended by other human figures. Another figure bearing a child in his or her arms may be connected with the custom of infant sacrifice, for which there is evidence in Neolithic Cyprus and in other countries of the Mediterranean. Finally a human figure is trying to climb over the wall of the sanctuary by the entrance, in an effort to see what is going on inside the *temenos*.

The importance of this object is multiple. First of all it is a bold artistic creation which called for skill and imagination on the part of the artist. It is an important piece of evidence on sacred architecture during a period for which up to now we do not possess any actual architectural remains. We know that open-air sanctuaries survived to a much later period in Cyprus (e.g., the sanctuary of Ayia Irini). But its greatest importance lies in the fact that it provides unique evidence on the Early Bronze Age religion of Cyprus. We have already come across the fertility goddess in the Chalcolithic idols of Erimi. Now we find more advanced religious ideas represented in the Vounous clay model. The figures in relief, probably cult images, wearing bull masks and holding snakes, are the central features of the ceremony and have significant attributes: the bull mask, the symbol of the god of fertility, and the snake, the symbol of the chthonian god. The kneeling figure has its arms outstretched as if in an attitude of prayer; the others have their arms crossed on their breasts. They are all seeking to partake of the power which is represented by the attributes, the bull and the snake. Both these symbols often appear in relief on vases of this period. One of them at least, the bull, survived for at least fifteen hundred years in Cypriote religion, always in association with the god of fertility. Another eloquent detail in this model is the figure trying to climb over the wall. In this humorous way the artist is telling us that the area within the enclosure of the *temenos* was a mystic precinct reserved for initiated members of the community.

Now for the first time in the early life of Cyprus we have abundant information about religious practices. Naturally the cycle of life and death impressed the Bronze Age Cypriot, who made it the basis of his religious conceptions. In order to render these two ideas more tangible he associated them with symbols, in the same way as the ancient Greeks several centuries later personified their religious ideas in the twelve Olympians.

The second object, also found in a tomb at Vounous, represents a ploughing scene. It shows two pairs of yoked oxen ploughing, each followed by a human figure; two other figures hold a piece of cloth containing grain, and another stands near a saddled animal. Though it was already known that the Cypriots had started ploughing the soil as early as the Neolithic period, we now have very vivid and tangible evidence on their method of ploughing—which is no different from that of the time of Hesiod, nor indeed from present-day Cyprus and other Near Eastern countries where similar ox-drawn wooden ploughs with metal ploughshares are still in use.

An attempt has been made to interpret an inscripting on the handle of a jug from Vounous as an alphabet. The suggestion has not, however, been generally accepted[58].

The fame of Cyprus as a copper-producing country must have spread by now to the whole of the Eastern Mediterranean. This would explain the material wealth of the Cypriots as seen in their tombs. This affluence may also explain the exuberance of their art and their elaborate religious practices.

Fortresses and Tombs of the Middle Bronze Age

This period is again mainly known from tombs, and therefore inadequately. Only one large house excavated at Kalopsidha, in the eastern part of the island, gives some information about trends in domestic architecture[59]. The house consists of a succession of eleven rectangular rooms built on three sides of a rectangle round a central courtyard. We know more about military architecture, which developed towards the end of the period owing

58. 59

60–62 →

63

64, 65

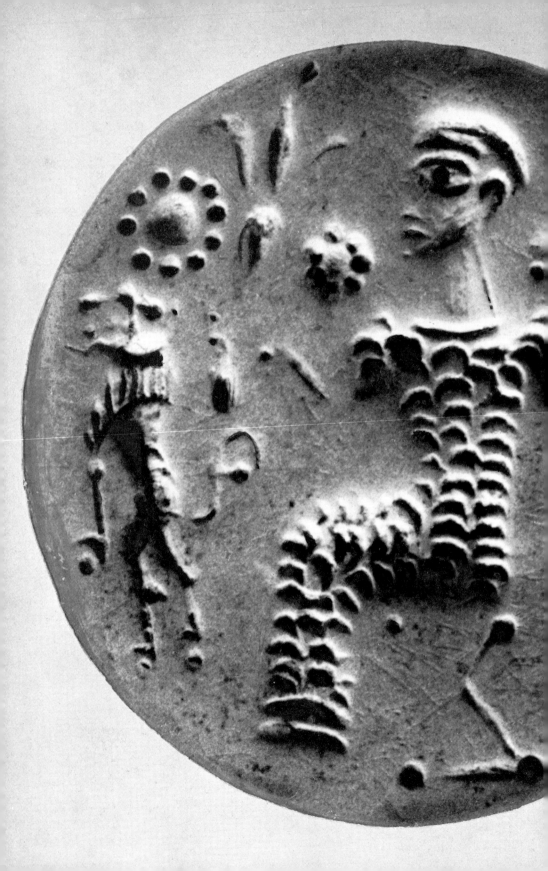

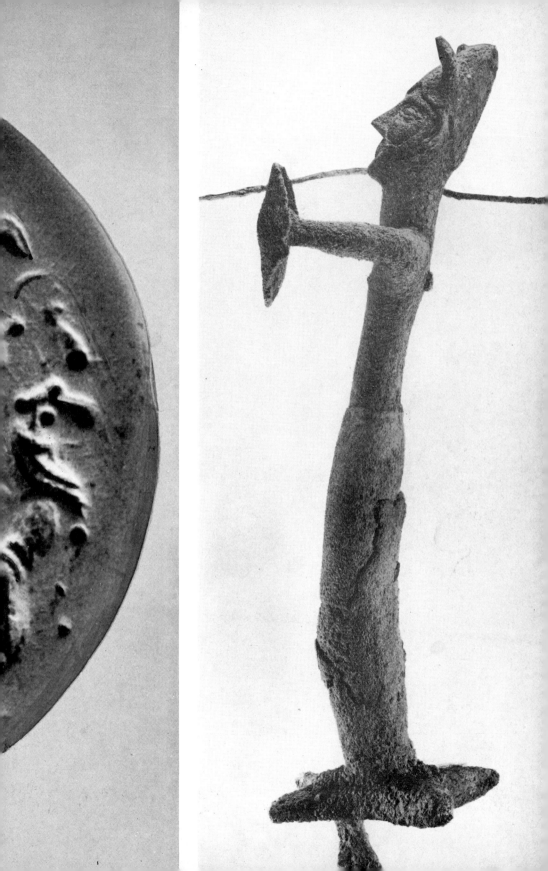

67–69

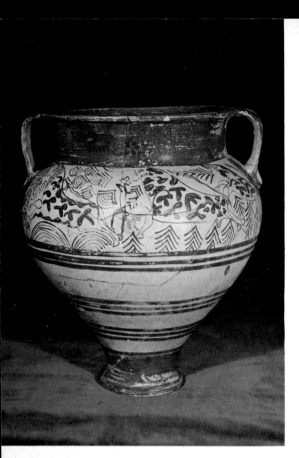

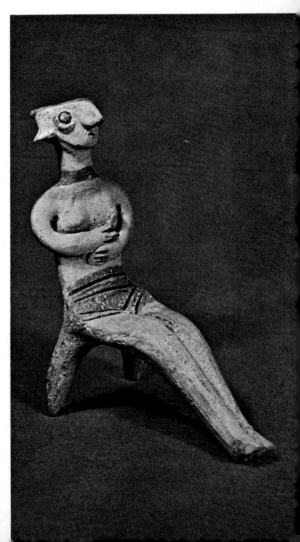

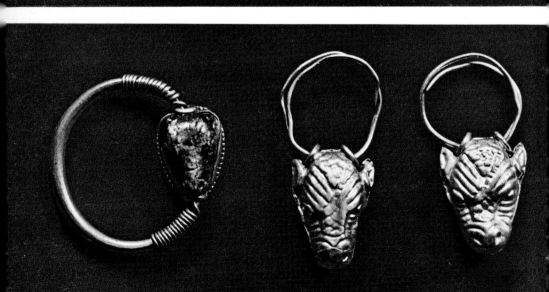

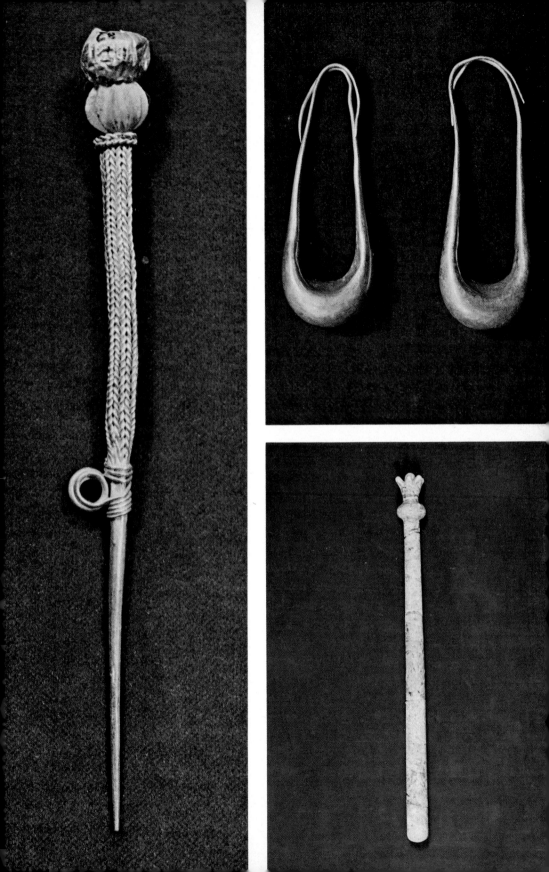

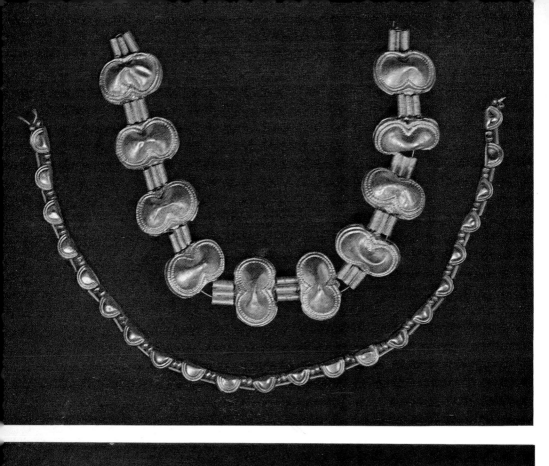

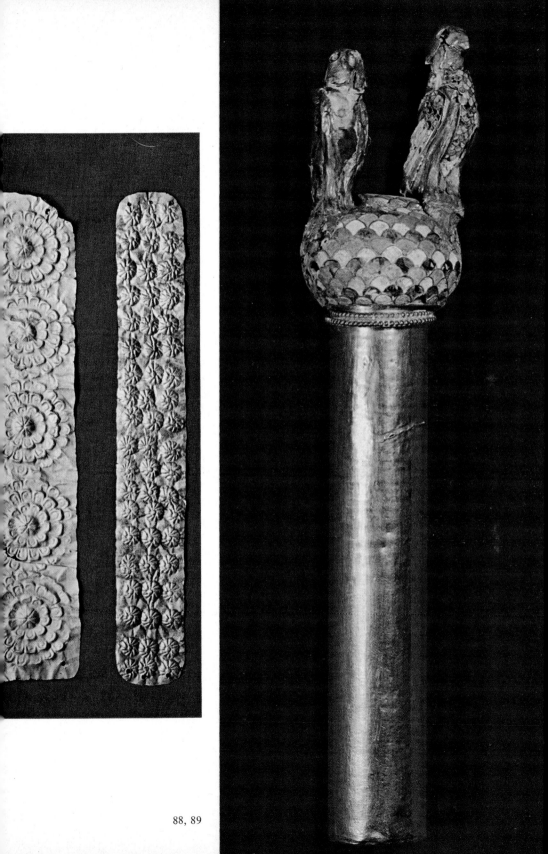

88, 89

93-95

to the atmosphere of war anxiety which prevailed in the Eastern Mediterranean as a result of internal unrest and the activities of the Hyksos. Fortresses of this period have recently been found along the northern coast,
the most prominent of them being the fortress at Krini, to the south of
the Kyrenia mountains[60]. Though it has not yet been excavated, its massive
northern wall of ashlar blocks, with solid bastions at regular intervals,
stands to a height of some 2 m. above ground; its south face has a strong
natural defence in the form of the unscaleable cliff above which the fortress
is built. Another fortress of the same period was discovered at Ayios Sozomenos, in the centre of the island. It has been suggested by Åström and
Catling that these fortresses were not built as a precaution against the raids
of seaborne enemies, but to guard against danger from within the island
itself during a period of serious internal unrest. Another fortress, Nitovikla,
on the south coast of the Karpass peninsula, dating from the end of the
Middle Bronze Age, has been connected with the raids of the Hyksos. It
has Anatolian elements in its architecture, recalling the fortifications of
Boğazköy. It consists of a rectangular courtyard enclosed by massive
walls, against which barracks were built, their flat roofs serving as plat-
forms for the guards. Two square towers flanked the entrance to the fortress.

Cemeteries have been discovered and excavated all over the island. Though
to a large extent the Early Bronze Age pattern of settlement continued
into the Middle Bronze Age, we now notice a shifting of importance from
the northern coast to the east and south, as discussed in Chapter I, with
Kalopsidha in the eastern part of the island as the most important centre.
Rich chamber tombs of the Middle Bronze Age have been excavated
throughout Cyprus. Their architecture shows an elaboration of Early
Bronze Age tomb structures, for instance in the Lapithos and Karmi
area, where a number of burial chambers are grouped round a common
passage or dromos. A unique feature is the relief of a human figure carved
on the wall of the dromos of a tomb recently discovered at Karmi by

J.R. Stewart (1960) excavating for the Melbourne Cyprus Expedition. This is the earliest funerary stele ever to be discovered in Cyprus. It is more than a metre high and is crudely carved. The façade of the chamber above the lintel is also carved to represent the exterior of a house. The idea of carving a figure in the dromos of a tomb may be related to Egyptian practices—e.g., the mastabas of the Old Kingdom, in which statues were placed for the same purpose. In another tomb, which dates from the early 18th century, a Kamares cup from Crete was also found *(Plate 55)*. The tomb is known as the "Tomb of the Seafarer"[61].

Tombs of a characteristic type occur at Palaeoskoutella close to the Nitovikla fortress which has already been mentioned. They may be compared with tombs found in Syria and Palestine, but they occur at this site for the first time in Cyprus. These innovations may suggest the presence of the Hyksos on the island some time in the 17th century.

Objects found in the Middle Bronze Age tombs show a ferment of artistic ideas, just as in the political and social field we notice an atmosphere of instability. The potter, having reached the peak of his achievement in the middle of the Early Bronze Age with Red Polished ware, now seeks new styles in a White Painted technique (painted linear motifs on a white ground). The vases are smaller than in the Early Bronze Age, but there is a striving to perfect the fabric and decoration. Plastically rendered figures often supplement the painted decoration *(Plates 53, 54)*. The usual tendency is to give the vase some of the attributes of a living creature, human or animal. Fantastic shapes are numerous, but often the potter confines himself to attributing facial characteristics to the upper part of the neck of a jug alone, thus giving the vase at least certain elements of a living creature. This is also found in the pottery of other countries in antiquity, including countries outside the Mediterranean area, for example Peru[62]. The ceramics of our own day, with Picasso in the lead, follow similar conceptions. Regional techniques also emerged, for instance the Red-on-

Black ware of Eastern Cyprus, but the White Painted technique was by far predominant.

Early in this period there were a few Minoan imports *(Plates 52, 53)*, but these are very rare and had no influence on Cypriote pottery[63]. Syro-Palestinian fabrics, however, are numerous towards the end of this period. Similarly Cypriote pottery of this period finds its way to Syria, Palestine and even Cilicia. Only very few fragments have been found in Crete during recent years; not enough yet to imply direct contacts[64].

Abundant bronze objects have been found in tombs, mainly daggers and tools developed from Early Bronze Age types. There are also a few imports from Crete and from the Syro-Palestinian coast.

The most significant event during the Middle Bronze Age is the growth of new centres of importance, with Kalopsidha in the east as the forerunner of the Late Bronze Age settlement of Enkomi. Through Kalopsidha a window to the East was opened, preparing Cyprus for the internationalism of the ensuing period.

Mycenaean Cyprus

Enkomi

The excitement caused by the discovery of the Neolithic culture in Cyprus was rivalled only by the impact of the discovery of Mycenaean Cyprus.

The Evidence of Excavation

Though the Late Bronze Age period had already been studied, along with the other archaeological periods, by Gjerstad and others in the twenties, it is only during the last twenty-five years or so that abundant light has been thrown on this period as a result of extensive excavations carried out by foreign expeditions and by the Cyprus Department of Antiquities. *Enkomi* is the most important of the Late Bronze Age sites. It was first discovered by looters who robbed a number of its tombs. Then a British expedition carried out further excavations in 1896, and thus enriched the British Museum collections of Mycenaean jewellery and Mycenaean pottery[65]. More tombs were excavated by the Swedish Cyprus Expedition in 1930[66]. The site had thus become known as the richest Late Cypriote necropolis on the island. Finally in 1934 Professor C.F.A. Schaeffer, who had been excavating the important Late Bronze Age site of Ras Shamra (Ugarit), on the Syrian coast opposite Cyprus, was led to Enkomi and with ingenuity and good fortune discovered that what had been regarded by all his predecessors as a necropolis was in fact a large city site, on which the tombs were in the courtyards of the houses and not in a separate cemetery. This was a sensational discovery: for the first time a whole Late Bronze Age city was available for excavation and study. Professor Schaeffer began excavations which, except for a break during the war, have continued every year, with very important results. In 1948 he invited the Cyprus Department of Antiquities to share the responsibility of excavation, and a joint French-Cypriote expedition was established with Dr P. Dikaios as the Cypriote component. This joint effort lasted for about eight years. Professor Schaeffer is now in sole charge of excavations on the site, on behalf of the French Centre National de la Recherche Scientifique[67].

Enkomi probably began as a small community at the end of the Middle Bronze Age, when Kalopsidha, some ten miles to the south-west, was the most important centre in eastern Cyprus. It lies in the plain below rocky cliffs which hide it from the sea. On its south side is the river Pedieos, which was probably once navigable from the sea up to this point. Tombs and scanty remains of houses from this period have been excavated, but the extent of the site cannot yet be determined. Enkomi, like the rest of the island, entered the Late Bronze Age (c. 1600 B.C.) in an atmosphere of unrest. The antagonism between the Hyksos of Asia Minor and the Egyptians had its repercussions in Cyprus. The destruction of the Middle Bronze Age fortress of Nitovikla (mentioned above, built in the 17th century), of Nikolidhes in the central part of Cyprus near Idalion (built at the beginning of the 16th century) and of Enkomi (built about 1550 and destroyed soon after), suggest that Cyprus did not remain free from the turmoil which agitated the Near East. The Hyksos most probably invaded and perhaps occupied the eastern part of Cyprus until they were expelled from the Eastern Mediterranean countries by the Egyptians. The peaceful conditions which prevailed in the Eastern Mediterranean after the expulsion of the Hyksos favoured the development of Cyprus. The copper mines were fully exploited and the metal was exported to the Near East from the harbour towns on the eastern and southern coasts of Cyprus. The northern part of the Enkomi site has produced substantial evidence for copper-smelting, especially in the partitions which were now built in the rooms.

While Cyprus was developing its commercial and cultural relations with the Syro-Palestinian coast, a new factor appeared in the Eastern Mediterranean which was destined to have a tremendous influence on the historical development of Cyprus. The Mycenaean Greeks, having become the predominant power in the Aegean after the "fall" of Knossos c. 1400 B.C., then expanded eastwards into the territory which had attracted the Minoans some three centuries earlier. Cyprus was an ideal place to use as a stepping-stone in their relations with the East. They traded with Syria and Palestine, having established themselves in the harbour towns on the east and south coasts of Cyprus. Enkomi was one of the leading centres to welcome these traders, who brought with them fine Mycenaean pottery and soon started making it on the spot, according to the styles of their homeland.

The Mycenaean Pottery of Cyprus

It is a controversial question whether the large quantities of Mycenaean pottery found in tombs of the early 14th century both in Cyprus and the Near East were all imported from the Greek mainland, or whether they were made in Cyprus by Mycenaean craftsmen. The present writer believes that among the traders there were also craftsmen who could produce Mycenaean pottery in Cyprus indistinguishable from the Mycenaean pottery of Greece. Side by side with purely Aegean shapes they imitated forms from the Cypriote repertoire, for instance the bowls with wishbone handles imitating Cypriote Base Ring and White Slip wares *(Plate 58)*, lentoid flasks, etc. The suggestion that these were made on the Greek mainland with the Cypriote market in mind may not be well founded. The quantity discovered has increased considerably during the last few years[68].

Favourite shapes were the large amphoroid and open craters which offered large surfaces for the application of the pictorial style of vase-painting *(Plates 70-72)*, which is best known from Mycenaean pottery found in Cyprus. The motifs and compositions were taken from the Aegean repertoire, but the style shows an exuberance which is not compatible with the severe style of mainland Mycenaean vase-painting and art in general. This is an additional argument in favour of a Cypriote origin for this spirited pictorial style, which must have been much favoured by the peoples of the Orient. Some fine craters decorated with chariot groups, bulls, birds and human figures, all in lively compositions, may be considered as among the finest specimens of Mycenaean art. Some scholars have even been able to identify mythological scenes in a number of such Mycenaean pictorial compositions[69].

Enkomi in particular has produced two such craters. One found by the Swedish Cyprus Expedition showed a chariot group and a long-robed human figure facing the horses and holding scales. This composition has been identified by the Swedish scholar Nilsson with the well-known Homeric scene in the *Iliad* in which Zeus holds the scales of destiny in front of the warriors before they depart for battle. Another crater recently discovered by Professor Schaeffer represents a chariot group with an enormous bird pursuing the figures in the chariot over the mountains *(Plate 71)*. This may represent a scene from Oriental mythology connected with the hunting and capture of a bird. Another crater found by Professor Schaeffer at Ras Shamra may represent an episode from the same myth. If these interpretations are correct, we thus have in the Mycenaean art of Cyprus the first elements of mythology as taken over by the Mycenaeans from Oriental sources. This is characteristic of the role which Cyprus played as an intermediary between the Aegean and the Orient.

The pictorial style in Mycenaean vase-painting from Cyprus—let us call this pottery Cypro-Mycenaean—had a long and interesting development throughout the 14th and 13th centuries. It was influenced at first by tapestry and weaving (Mycenaean IIIB style) and produced scenes with animals like bulls, goats and birds, drawn in outline and filled in with small motifs derived from tapestry. They are more notable for decorative than for representational qualities, but fit admirably on to the surface of vases *(Plate 73)* such as bell craters and shallow bowls. Towards the end of the 13th century a new style made its appearance in Cypro-Mycenaean vase-painting, influenced by the art of carving, probably ivory carving[70]. Thick and thin lines are used for outlining the figures, and thin lines for rendering anatomical details within the body outline. This is the first attempt in Greek art at real drawing as we know it later from Attic vase-painting. Enkomi has produced some of the finest examples, for instance the bell crater showing a bull and a goat near a bush, in a lively composition. This vase was found by the Swedish Cyprus Expedition. This style, however, bearing the unhappy name of "Rude Style", soon degenerated as the peaceful conditions in the Near East began—as we shall see below— to give way to turmoil once more.

Gold and Silver Objects

In addition to the pottery Enkomi has produced one of the most remarkable silver bowls known in Mycenaean art. It was found by Professor Schaeffer in a 14th century tomb *(Plate 75)*[71]. It is decorated in the inlaid technique which is also known from the shaft graves of Mycenae: on the outer surface of the bowl is a frieze of bucrania and stylised flowers, inlaid in gold and niello. A similar bowl is known from Dendra in the Peloponnese, but the Enkomi bowl is much superior.

Other objects found in the Enkomi tombs include gold diadems with impressed decoration, jewellery of all kinds *(Plates 86, 87)*, ivory and faience objects, cylinder seals, bronze and alabaster vases, etc. Indeed the wealth of the tombs of Enkomi is rivalled only by the tombs of Mycenae. Many of the objects mentioned above show a definite influence of Mycenaean art (particularly conspicuous in glyptic art), but Oriental elements are always present. In fact we are entitled to talk of an Aegeo-Oriental style during the 14th and 13th centuries which had Cyprus as a centre[72]. Enkomi has yielded the most numerous and finest specimens of this style.

During the last quarter of the 13th century important events occurred at Enkomi. The excavations have revealed a conspicuous layer of destruction throughout the city, which is associated with pottery known as Mycenaean IIIC:1, of a type which was imported from the Argolid *(Plate 96)*. The city was soon rebuilt on an entirely new plan. An impressive cyclopean wall was built round it, consisting of two parallel rows of large blocks of stone 3 m. thick at the base, with a superstructure of mud bricks. Rectangular towers were built at intervals along the city wall. One large tower was built beside the northern gate.

Architecture

The city wall has been traced for its complete course, and we now know the full extent of the city. Its maximum length from north to south is

c. 400 m., and the distance from the wall on the west side to the cliffs which formed the eastern limit of the town is c. 350 m. The street grid of the new town is remarkably regular. In the northern half this forms a uniform pattern, with seven east-west streets, 3 m. wide, at regular intervals of 32 m.; these are crossed by one north-south street, the northern end of which is aligned on the north gate. The southern part of the town has a different grid. At the intersection of two main streets near the centre of the town is a square paved with stone slabs, near which are public buildings.

The site of the small houses built of rubble and mud bricks is now occupied by impressive public buildings of considerable size built of large ashlar blocks in a style which recalls the finest works of classical Greek architecture. A number of such buildings have been revealed at Enkomi, the largest being the so-called "Bâtiment 18" excavated by Professor Schaeffer *(Plate 67)*. It has a long and impressive façade with a central doorway and large windows. The ashlar architecture is of the Oriental tripartite type, but there are also features of the Mycenaean megaron-type architecture. "Bâtiment 18" is thought to have been the residence of an Achaean aristocrat. Other public buildings constructed in ashlar include sanctuaries, of which two have been discovered. One of them *(Plate 68)* was excavated by Dr Dikaios (the sanctuary which produced the statue of the first Horned God – *Plate 95);* it is of the tripartite type, with a rectangular recess in the central part where the bronze statue was found. Another sanctuary excavated by Professor Schaeffer consists of a vestibule in front of the main cella, in the centre of which there is a stone pillar which supported the roof.

The changes at Enkomi which followed its destruction—the building of a cyclopean wall, the new town layout, the public buildings constructed in ashlar, and the appearance of a new style of pottery (Mycenaean IIIC:1)— have been associated with the arrival in Cyprus of Achaean colonists from the Peloponnese, following the disaster which befell its leading centres like

Mycenae and Pylos towards the end of the 13th century. Apart from changes in material culture there were also other profounder changes which marked the beginning of the hellenisation of the island.

Sculpture

The discovery of the bronze statue of the Horned God in one of the main sanctuaries of the city shows that new religious ideas were also being introduced[73]. The Horned God *(Plate 95)* may be identified with Apollo Kereatas of Arcadia in Greece, who survived with this name in another part of the island down to the Hellenistic period. The statue, 55 cm. high, is of solid construction and must have stood on a base of some different material. It was almost certainly a cult statue; near the place where it was found there were skulls of oxen and a large quantity of bowls, evidently used during ritual ceremonies. The god is young, wearing a short kilt and a conical helmet with bulls' horns in front. The left arm is bent, with fist clenched against the chest; the right arm is bent forward, with the palm of the hand turned downwards. The youthful god has fine facial characteristics which recall in many ways the style of archaic Greek sculpture. The date of the statue may be early in the 12th century.

A smaller bronze statue 35 cm. high, of a slightly later date, has recently been found in yet another sanctuary by Professor Schaeffer *(Plate 65)*[74]. The sanctuary has also yielded large terracotta figures of two-headed centaurs, of Cretan inspiration, dating from the early 11th century, and large numbers of bucrania. The god is standing on an ingot. He is bearded, and wears a horned helmet and a short tunic, with greaves on his legs. With his right hand he brandishes a spear, and in his left he holds a small round shield. Professor Schaeffer believes that he is the god who protected the copper mines of Cyprus. The style of this statue is less refined than the youthful Horned God, but of equal quality. These two statues are not only valuable evidence for the study of religion, but are also works of art of high quality, especially notable at a time when bronze statuettes are usually not larger than 15–20 cm. *(Plate 94)*.

Contemporary with the bronze statues are a number of ivories from Enkomi found in 1896 by the British Museum expedition. They date from the early part of the 12th century and show clear Mycenaean and Oriental features. The best known is the game-box now in the British Museum, with representations in relief of the hunting of bulls and wild goats from a chariot on the two long sides, and of bulls lying near olive trees on one of the short sides. Also from Enkomi are two mirror handles with carved relief representations of a lion attacking a bull and a hero attacking a griffin[75].

The Sea Peoples and the Decline of Enkomi

There is abundant evidence at Enkomi for an extensive destruction soon after the general rebuilding which followed the arrival of the first Achaean colonists. Similar destructions have been observed in other Cypriote towns at the same period, and are generally considered to be the result of raids by the so-called Sea Peoples. The impressive buildings constructed of ashlar blocks which have been described above were repaired and reinhabited, but the city seems to have lost the splendour of the earlier period; the arrival of new settlers, both from the Levant and from the Aegean, after the Dorian invasion (the latter bringing with them the Mycenaean IIIC:2 pottery), did not succeed in reviving the city. At about the year 1075 B.C. an earthquake gave the final blow to the town, and indeed to most of the Late Bronze Age cities of Cyprus. The inhabitants of Enkomi started moving towards the sea and built Salamis near the estuary of the river Pedieos, where a new harbour town was destined to flourish as the capital of Cyprus. The discovery at Salamis of early 11th century remains indicates that for a period of about twenty-five years the two coexisted, until Enkomi was finally abandoned towards the middle of the 11th century, never to be rebuilt. The silting up of its harbour may have been another reason for this definitive abandonment[76].

Kition

Kition, a site with a natural harbour and one of a chain of harbour towns along the south coast of Cyprus, appears on the cultural scene quite early in the Bronze Age[77]. Tombs dating from the end of the Early Bronze Age have been found on the site which was later to develop as a Late Bronze Age town, but nothing has been discovered of the settlement of this early period. Sherds of the Middle Bronze Age suggest a continuity of occupation, but the actual remains of a town do not date, so far as our present evidence goes, earlier than the 14th century.

The modern town of Larnaca is built over the Bronze Age remains, and therefore excavation over a large area is not possible. Two building plots in the centre of the town and a fairly large strip of land along the ancient city wall will, however, provide ample evidence when they have been completely excavated. In one of the plots in the centre of the town (Area I) excavation has been completed, and a clear picture of the history of the town has been obtained. The Late Cypriote II houses were built on top of the Early Bronze Age tombs. Their plan was like that of the houses at Enkomi, that is L-shaped with a courtyard in front. The family tombs were hewn from the rock in the courtyard of the house—again as at Enkomi. Some chamber tombs were used successively for a number of burials down to the end of the 13th century. Three such tombs have been excavated and the material discovered in them shows that they are by no means inferior in wealth to the Enkomi tombs.

Wealth and Commercial Importance

In fact the quantity of gold, ivory and faience objects found in Tomb 9 cannot be equalled by any other Late Cypriote tomb so far known *(Plates 82, 88)*.

The finds included more than a dozen gold diadems decorated with embossed ornaments, gold rings, ear-rings, bowls and flasks of Egyptian faience decorated with floral ornaments, bronzes, alabaster vases *(Plate 90)*, ivory objects including a miniature bath, and large quantities of Mycenaean vases, quite outnumbering the local Cypriote ware. Egyptian or Egyptianising objects form a large proportion of the small finds; apart from the faience and alabaster vases there were also cornelian beads of Egyptian type, scarabs, Egyptianising jewellery, ostrich eggs, and cylinder seals showing obvious Egyptian influence in their designs *(Plates 61, 62)*.

Large quantities of copper slag found on the floors of the houses, as well as of clay pipes and crucibles, leave no doubt that copper was smelted at Kition, as at Enkomi, during the 14th and 13th centuries. In fact the copper mines of Kalavassos and Troulli are nearer Kition than Enkomi. Considering the Egyptian imports and the Egyptian influence in the objects found in the Kition tombs, the fact that Kition is open to the Egyptian sea, and also that copper was smelted in this harbour town in southern Cyprus, its claim to be the ancient Alasia is surely at least as good as that of Enkomi—if indeed this name is to be assigned to a particular town and not to the island as a whole. Like Enkomi, Kition could, and very probably did, send copper to the Pharaoh, to whom, according to the Amarna tablets, the king of Alasia had to remit an annual tribute of copper.

The second tomb at Kition (Area I) has produced an extraordinary object—though, as we shall see, it was found outside the chamber as a result of pillaging in antiquity. It is a conical rhyton *(Plates 76, 77)*, almost complete, 28 cm. high, made of thick faience, covered inside and outside with a thick layer of blue enamel and decorated in a very unusual technique. Its outer surface is divided by horizontal lines into three registers, the upper and middle registers being filled with animal and human figures and the lowest with vertical rows of running spirals. The three animals in the uppermost register are represented at full gallop among stylised flowers— a bull, inlaid in red enamel, a calf, painted in yellow, and a wild goat, also in yellow. All the figures are outlined in black. In the middle register are two groups of bull-hunters, the human figures being inlaid in red enamel and the animal figures painted in yellow. Stylised flowers in yellow and red again fill in the background. The spirals are painted yellow. The figure drawing is lively and realistic; the compositions are reminiscent of the decoration of the Vaphio cups from the Peloponnese, but also of motifs from Egyptian reliefs and tomb paintings. The bearded human figures with their kilts and conical helmets are Oriental in character. The galloping animals with their backward-turned heads are characteristic of Aegean art but were also common in Oriental art at a much earlier date. The spiral is an Aegean motif, as is also the form of the rhyton itself. There is no doubt that this object is an Oriental product, made either in Cyprus or in some Syro-Palestinian centre. It was made either by a Mycenaean or an Oriental artist, under the influence of the so-called Aegeo-Oriental style, in which Aegean and Oriental elements were fused. This "international" style was prevalent in the Near East throughout the 14th and 13th centuries. Our rhyton cannot be dated exactly, but a terminal date not later that c. 1230 can be accepted.

Tomb 9 at Kition yielded valuable evidence on the destruction of the city at the end of the 13th century. The last burial contained ceramic material which can be dated to the very end of the Mycenaean IIIB style, being almost identical with that from Tomb 18 at Enkomi (Swedish Cyprus Expedition), which was used for the last time either shortly before or shortly after the catastrophe which coincided with the arrival of the first Achaean colonists[78]. At Kition this destruction was even more violent than at Enkomi. The Late Cypriote II houses were levelled up, and upon their foundations and fallen mud bricks a layer of clayey soil was strewn to make a foundation for the construction of the new city *(Plate 16)*. These new houses had thick walls, well built, in one case with ashlar blocks. It should be remembered that the excavation described here does not exceed the area of a building plot, so that very little can be said about the architecture of the new buildings or the layout of the new town. Inside and upon the floors of these houses Mycenaean IIIC:1 pottery was found, a fact which brings together the history of Kition and Enkomi. Kition, like Enkomi, must have received Achaean colonists who rebuilt the town on a completely new plan.

Soon afterwards, however, these houses were destroyed, probably by the Sea Peoples as at Enkomi. Mycenaean IIIC:2 pottery found on the new floors of the rebuilt or repaired houses suggests the arrival towards the end of the 12th century of new waves of Achaean colonists. The city was again destroyed by some natural force, probably an earthquake, during the second quarter of the 11th century. On the débris of the fallen walls, however, new houses were built with massive walls and thick floors, or old houses were repaired and inhabited during the early Geometric period. This occupation did not last long. The dwellings were suddenly abandoned c. 1000 B.C. for a reason which has not yet been determined. The city must have moved nearer the sea, as at Salamis, probably as a result of the silting up of the inner navigable channel of the harbour. The possible arrival during this period of the first Phoenician colonists, who established themselves near the sea, may have encouraged the transfer of the city's centre nearer the sea.

History of the Town

A larger area has been excavated near the northern part of the city wall (Area II). It has been ascertained that by the Late Cypriote II period

(c. 14th century) Kition was already a fortified city *(Plates 56, 57)*. Its walls more or less followed the natural formation of the ground, i.e., the perimeter of the low plateau on which the city was built. This early wall was built of sun-dried bricks on a small rubble foundation. At intervals there were substantial rectangular bastions, two of which have been cleared. The first of these measures 13.50 m. in width and 5 m. in depth, and the second 18.50 m. in width and 5 m. in depth. One of them is preserved to a height of 2.30 m. We ascertained that these bastions, of which the foundations lie at least 2.50 m. lower than the foundations of the city wall proper, were washed by the marshes or by shallow sea-water in antiquity. The excavations, carried out during the driest months of the year, nevertheless reached water level at the foundations. The advantages of this system for the defence of the city are obvious, and recall much later mediaeval practices.

The mud brick wall was destroyed during the turmoil at the end of the 13th century. It was replaced by a large cyclopean wall like that at Enkomi, which was built immediately on top of the fallen débris of mud bricks from the previous wall. Its thickness was 2.40 m., and it has now been excavated for a length of about 100 m. It consisted at its base of two parallel rows of large blocks of stone, while the upper part was of mud brick. The bastions were retained, after repairs, but a new feature now appears, a street adjacent to the city wall, measuring c. 3 m. in width, passing outside the bastions. The tracks of chariot wheels are still visible on the surface of the street *(Plate 56)*.

Some time at the beginning of the 11th century the city was destroyed, probably by an earthquake, as we have already seen in Area I. The cyclopean city wall collapsed and its mud bricks fell on to the street to the north, forming a thick layer which was never removed. In the early Geometric period houses were built on top of this layer outside the city wall. Other houses were built upon the remains of the earlier houses inside the walls, but in some cases the foundations of the houses of the previous period were re-used. As in Area I, here too we have evidence of a short period of habitation, after which (c. 1000 B.C.) this part of the city was abandoned.

Other Late Bronze Age Sites

Various other sites of the Late Bronze Age have been excavated throughout the island—e.g., at Kourion (Bamboula), Palaeokastro-Maa (Paphos district), Sinda (Famagusta district), Myrtou (Kyrenia district), Kokkinokremnos (Larnaca district), and Idalion (Nicosia district).

Kourion–Bamboula

Kourion-Bamboula, which lies a short distance east of the classical city site of Kourion, was excavated in 1937 and 1939 by an American expedition from the University Museum, Philadelphia, under the direction of Dr J.F. Daniel. Within a circuit of defensive walls a complex of houses and streets was found. At Palaeokastro-Maa Dr P. Dikaios, excavating in 1954 for the Cyprus Department of Antiquities, cleared part of a city wall like that at Enkomi, intended to protect the landward side of a settlement lying on a peninsula with steep cliffs on the seaward side *(Plate 14)*.

Myrtou–Pigadhes

At Myrtou-Pigadhes a sanctuary was excavated by a British expedition led by Miss Joan du Plat Taylor in 1952[79]. Apart from the buildings of the sanctuary, an interesting feature at Myrtou was an altar built of ashlar blocks of limestone, probably—according to the excavator's reconstruction—with "horns of consecration". The altar was built in the 13th century and destroyed at the beginning of the 12th century.

The Sceptre of Kaloriziki

To the very end of the Late Bronze Age belongs the cemetery of Kaloriziki at Kourion, where Mycenaean type chamber tombs with long narrow dromoi were found, similar to those at Lapithos. One of these tombs, which was probably a royal tomb, yielded a gold sceptre-head 16.5 cm. high, of exquisite workmanship *(Plate 89)*[80]. This probably belonged to the sceptre of a king, a token of his authority according to the usage recorded in Homer. It consists of a gold tube upon which are two hawks perched on a cloisonné sphere. The compartments are filled with green, white and mauve enamel, a rare technique which was for long considered to date from a much later period. Other material in the same tomb, including bronze weapons, vessels and tripod stands, dates the burial and therefore the sceptre to c. 1050 B.C.

Salamis and the Archaic Period of Cyprus

From the 11th century onwards Cypriote archaeology and history are dominated by *Salamis*[81]. The city site and the necropolis of Salamis have been intensively investigated during recent years, and the results of these researches will be briefly described below.

Excavation and History of the Site

We have already referred in Chapter I to the importance of the discoveries made in 1965 by the French archaeological mission from the University of Lyons, headed by Professor J. Pouilloux[82]. Near the harbour area of Salamis, round which the early city must have been built after the abandonment of Enkomi, floors of houses were found near the bed-rock, associated with Proto-White Painted Ware sherds of the first half of the 11th century B.C. A chamber tomb of the same period was discovered a short distance to the west of the harbour area. In this tomb more than two hundred and fifty vases were found *(Plate 63)*, as well as jewellery, including finger rings, rosettes and a fine gold needle. A *kalathos* from this tomb is decorated with a wild goat, a rare motif for this period which was taken over from Cretan sub-Minoan vase-painting.

Salamis must have started as a small harbour town, and its necropolis, as noted above, was not far from its western limits. Later, however, in the 8th century B.C., when the city expanded in all directions, the old necropolis area was built over, and a new necropolis established much farther west, in the area which is now bounded by the western limits of the Salamis forest and the Monastery of St Barnabas. The gap between the 11th and the 8th centuries has not been filled. This represents the Dark Age of Cypriote archaeology, but intensive excavation on the site of Salamis will surely establish a continuous sequence. The situation here is characteristic of the whole island: only a few cemeteries are known but no settlements.

Large built tombs have been excavated at Salamis dating from the 8th to the 7th centuries, throwing abundant light on the history of the period, the material culture and the burial customs. The first tomb was excavated in 1957 *(Plate 136)* by Dr. P. Dikaios for the Cyprus Department of Antiquities[83], but since 1962 many more tombs have been investigated by the present writer, also for the Department of Antiquities.

The main characteristic of the tombs now to be described is the large dromos in front of the chamber, in which, in addition to amphorae and other vases, skeletons of horses and remains of chariots have been found.

The Chariot Tombs

Tomb 47 was excavated in 1964. Its rectangular funerary chamber *(Plate 113)*, built of large ashlar blocks, had been looted long ago, but the dromos remained intact. Its sloping cement floor measured 20 m. in length and 13.65 m. in maximum width. The dromos leads up to a paved propylaeum by a flight of four steps of good quality masonry. The propylaeum is in the form of the Greek letter L, and behind this is the chamber. On the cement floor close to the propylaeum the skeletons of two yoked horses were found. The yoke and the pole of the waggon which they had been drawing had left their impressions in the soil, but the waggon itself was not found; possibly it was detachable and was placed within the chamber with the body upon it, as in central European burials. The horses were fully harnessed, with leather blinkers and frontlets covered with thin sheets of gold. The iron bits were found in the horses' mouths. The animals had obviously been sacrificed in honour of the dead man after his body had been laid in the chamber.

Vases found in the dromos dated this burial to the late 8th century. Towards the middle of the 7th century the same tomb was re-used by cutting a passage through the filling of the dromos of the first burial to provide access to the *stomion* of the chamber. In this passage, about a metre above the floor of the dromos, six horses were sacrificed in honour of the dead man. They were yoked in pairs, and had blinkers and frontlets of ivory and bronze *(Plate 125)*. The pottery included some unusual forms—for example a stand with a long stem consisting of two nude female figures painted red *(Plate 145)*. The sacrifice of horses in honour of the dead is an Oriental custom which was known in Mycenaean Greece and is mentioned by Homer.

Not far from Tomb 47 another tomb of almost identical construction (Tomb 50) was excavated in 1965. This is the so-called Prison or Tomb of St Catherine, a megalithic monument which has been described by many travellers from the 14th century onwards *(Plate 114)*. The excavation of the dromos (28 m. in length and 13 m. in maximum width) revealed two skeletons of yoked horses *(Plate 115)*, and pottery dating from the 7th century B.C. There is some probability that the tomb may also have been used at an earlier date, but subsequent disturbances of the filling of the dromos from the Roman period onwards had left only very scanty remains of the original material. Both sides of the dromos are faced with ashlar blocks. The façade of the chamber, 3.40 m. high with a cornice at the top on all three sides, is built of very large blocks of stone, some of them measuring $4 \times 2.50 \times 1$ m. The chamber, consisting of two enormous blocks placed one above the other, had a gable roof.

In the Roman period there were various changes in this tomb, involving the transformation of the propylaeum into a vaulted chamber for an unidentifiable purpose.

Tomb 79 and its Treasures

The richest tomb so far excavated at Salamis, and one of the richest on the whole island, is Tomb 79, which was excavated in 1966. The tomb chamber, like that of Tomb 50, had been robbed in Roman times when it was re-used as a tomb, but the filling of the long sloping dromos (20 m. long and about 13 m. wide) remained intact *(Plate 118)*. Stratigraphic evidence showed that there were two burials, the first at the end of the 8th century B.C., and the second soon afterwards, probably at the very beginning of the 7th century; and this was confirmed by the objects discovered and by their disposition in the dromos.

Four chariots were found on the floor of the dromos; two of them belonged to the first burial, and had been moved to the left side of the dromos in order to make room for two other chariots belonging to the second burial. The skeletons of the horses associated with the chariots of the first burial had been disturbed at the time of the removal and were found mixed with the soil filling, but those of the second burial were found *in situ (Plate 119)*, yoked to their chariots. The first of the two chariots of the first burial has two poles, and is more or less complete, with its yoke *in situ (Plate 20)*. The wood has left clear impressions in the soil, and all the metal parts have been preserved. It had a small chariot box, most probably made of osiers, divided into two compartments. At the back of the chariot box a large bronze loop was found, which had been fixed at the middle of the back of the chariot in order to help in mounting the chariot. The ten-spoked wheels did not have metal tyres, but there were iron nails corresponding to each of the spokes. Two imposing linch–pins were found *in situ*, consisting of a bronze sphinx's head through the iron pin, and the figure of an armed soldier above the sphinx's head *(Plate 122)*. The total length is 56 cm., making them unique in size in the Near East. The soldier is hollow inside and served as a rattle. He wears a short tunic and a foliated cuirass, which is inlaid with blue glass. His helmet recalls certain Assyrian prototypes; the crest on top of it has holes for feathers (?). There is a sword hanging on a strap from his shoulder, and he is holding the pommel. The soldier's eyes as well as the disc of his helmet above the forehead are inlaid with blue glass.

The second chariot is poorly preserved. Only the box has been found, with no wheels, though the axle is clearly visible. The chariot box was decorated all round with five large lions' heads in bronze.

Of the two chariots belonging to the second burial one is well preserved, with the two skeletons of horses *in situ*. The horses have all their metal gear *in situ*—bronze frontal bands and blinkers, bronze breast-plates and side pendant ornaments (the disc-shaped ornament which is usually seen above the horse's forelegs on chariots in Assyrian reliefs) and iron bits.

The yoke of the chariot is decorated with four bronze standards in the shape of a flower *(Plate 123)*. We are now certain about their original position, and in this respect they may well be compared with those on the gold Persian chariot from the Oxus Treasure.

The yoke and the horses of the second chariot were partly damaged by stone robbers who disturbed the filling of the dromos at the entrance when they dug for stones from the sides of the dromos.

In the north corner of the propylaeum near the façade of the chamber was a pile of bronze and iron objects consisting of the bronze gear of the horses belonging to the two chariots of the first burial. The breast-plates, side pendant ornaments, blinkers and frontal bands are all decorated with figured representations *(Plates 121, 124)* which show affinities with Assyrian works of art.

We may particularly mention the breast-plates, which are entirely covered with animal and human figures from the Assyrian repertoire. The side pendant ornaments portray the nude goddess Ishtar, standing on two lions' backs and holding lions in her hands, thus recalling the Greek *potnia therôn*.

An item of particular importance is a pair of iron firedogs, 1.10 m. long, terminating at either end in the prow and stern of a ship, not unlike those found at Palaepaphos in 1963 and at Argos in the Peloponnese[84]. The appearance of yet another pair of these objects in an identical shape, as part of a warrior's tomb furniture, may not be fortuitous. In another part of the dromos, not far from the firedogs, was a bundle of twelve iron skewers, 1.50 m. long.

Other notable objects found on the floor of the tomb were two bronze cauldrons *(Plate 120)*. One of these, standing on an iron tripod, was decorated round the rim with eight protomes of griffins and four double-faced bird-men or sphinxes, crested and bearded. This cauldron is of importance both as a work of art and because it throws new light on the problem of the origin of other such cauldrons found in Etruria and in Greece. This cauldron was completely filled with clay juglets from the first burial. The second cauldron, standing on a high conical base, has two horizontal loop handles, with three bull protomes below them fixed at the rim. Below each of the handles, on the body of the vessel itself, is a plaque decorated with a large Hathor head between two fan-shaped motifs in the Egyptianising style.

These metal objects may have been made in Cyprus, but under strong North Syrian and ultimately Urartian influence.

Apart from the metal objects this tomb also yielded objects of ivory *(Plate 133)*, which again were in a pile near the northern corner of the propylaeum and belonged to the first burial. The most important of these are two thrones, both made of wood (now perished) and finely decorated. One was faced with plaques of silver, ivory and blue glass; of these only the oxidised silver plaques had left their traces on the soil, the rest being found on the floor. The other was decorated with plain plaques of ivory alternating with carved ones in guilloche motifs *(Plate 134)*. The upper part of the back was covered with a thin sheet of gold. There were also inlaid friezes of small anthemia consisting of separate small pieces of ivory. Near the first throne was a footstool; near the other were the dismembered parts of a large ivory bed. Only one of its legs, of solid ivory, has been found; but to this bed may belong a number of long narrow ivory panels, undecorated, and of carved plaques, with antithetic sphinxes on either side of a tree motif (the sphinxes are partly gilded) *(Plate 129)* or with the well-known representation of Heh holding a palm branch from which hangs the *ankh* symbol *(Plate 130)*. Various parts of the composition are gilded. One of the most beautiful of the ivory plaques is carved on both sides in the form of a winged and crowned sphinx *(Plate 127)*. The wings, etc., are carved into compartments, the walls of which have a thin coating of gold, the compartments themselves being filled with blue and brown (?) paste. Another object in the same technique is a plaque representing a composite flower *(Plate 128)*. One very unusual item is an ivory object

111, 112

in the shape of an incense-burner *(Plate 131)*, with three rows of super-imposed drooping leaves and three thin outward-curving "legs". Such objects are usually found only in bronze *(Plate 126)*.

The ivories are of good quality, and may well be compared with those from Nimrud. No doubt they were imported, probably from Syria. They may be called Phoenician, in the Egyptianising style, which was the *koine* for ivory carving in Syria and Palestine during the 8th and 7th centuries.

Large quantities of pottery were found on the floor of the dromos, especially along the two sides. This included large amphorae, both painted and plain, and also numerous dishes, many of them containing fish and chicken bones. Considerable numbers of murex shells were also found.

The pottery dates the first burial the to very end of the 8th century B.C. The ivory thrones and other plaques, and the cauldrons and the objects found piled up in the corner near the façade, also belong to this burial. The second burial was poorer. Apart from the two chariots we may attribute to it only pottery (mainly large bowls and dishes containing food). The chronological interval between the two burial periods, however, must be reckoned as very short—no more than a few years. The fact that at least one of the chariots from the first burial was wheeled away, and that most of the furniture (thrones, bed, etc.) could be moved away into a corner shows that these objects were still in fairly good condition at the time of the second burial. This is also shown by the fact that the gear associated with the horses of the two periods is almost identical.

The tomb which we have briefly described may be considered one of the richest, if not the richest, ever found in Cyprus. The wealth of its ivories and bronzes shows how rich and powerful were the kings of Salamis, no less important in their material possessions than their continental counterparts.

Other Important Tombs

Smaller built tombs of the 7th century were found in the same area. Tombs 19 and 31 had two asses sacrificed in their dromoi instead of horses, neither having any metal gear on them. Tomb 31 was found intact. On its floor was an amphora containing the incinerated remains of the dead man (a rare custom at Salamis, where inhumation was the usual practice). A large number of gold diadems rolled into a ball were found in a pit on the floor of the chamber. They are decorated in repoussé with chariot groups *(Plate 135)*, sphinxes and rosettes.

In the dromos of Tomb 2 (excavated in 1962) remains of a chariot and the skeletons of two asses were found on the floor of the dromos *(Plates 116, 117)*, together with large amphorae. Inside the partly looted chamber a silver bowl was found. The inside of the bowl had been decorated twice, the second decoration being superimposed on the other after the first had faded. The first decoration consisted of a central medallion containing two human figures encircled by zones filled with floral and linear motives, including a long pseudo-hieroglyphic inscription. The second decoration, in a similar arrangement, consisted of a central medallion occupied by a winged sphinx and enriched by zones filled with linear motifs and antithetically arranged winged sphinxes.

The style of both decorations shows strong Egyptian elements, but the artist may have been a Phoenician working in Cyprus.

In the dromos of the tomb evidence of human sacrifice was obtained, recalling a similar practice observed in an early Iron Age tomb at Lapithos near the northern coast. Tomb 2 was used twice, in the 8th and the 7th centuries, according to stratigraphic observations and the evidence of the pottery.

A late 7th century tomb was excavated in 1964 (Tomb 3). It is a built tomb surmounted by a large tumulus of earth some 60 m. in diameter and 10 m. in height. The tomb had been looted by villagers at some time in the past.

In 1890 British archaeologists had tunnelled through and destroyed a large part of the dromos, but enough survived for us when we reinvestigated it. Remains of two chariots and four horses were found. In the box of one of the chariots was a silver-studded sword, 92 cm. long, in its sheath *(Plate 132)*, with its ivory toggle and leather strap. Among the large amphorae found on either side of the dromos was one bearing a painted inscription in the Cypriote syllabary containing the word "of olive oil", giving a clear indication of its original contents. For Homeric scholars this recalls the description of the funeral of Patroclus in the *Iliad*, when amphorae of olive oil and honey were put near the pyre.

The tumulus was crowned at its top with a beehive construction of mud bricks, 8.60 m. in diameter at the base. It may have been built to recall an earlier Mycenaean fashion in tomb architecture, such as is known from the beehive tombs at Mycenae and from the two recently discovered examples at Enkomi—providing another example of the conservative character of the Cypriots.

Another part of the Salamis necropolis, the Cellarka site, has examples of rock-cut tombs belonging to ordinary people. They are hewn from the hard surface rock, and have a stepped dromos leading down to a rectangular chamber with a flat or saddle roof. The boundaries of the tombs are indicated on the surface by walls of ashlar blocks *(Plate 148)*. The tombs were used repeatedly from the end of the 8th century down to the 4th century B.C. Unusual burial customs have been observed which recall Greek funerary customs, for instance the offering of a pyre in the dromos of the tomb, on which in addition to small vases and terracotta figurines were placed cereals and fruit, mainly figs, almonds and grapes *(Plates 137, 147, 152)*. This custom, known as *pankarpia* or *panspermia* in ancient Greek religion, has survived in the modern Greek world in the offering of *kollyva* in honour of the dead.

The Cellarka tombs yielded considerable quantities of Eastern Greek pottery, another indication of the second Greek colonisation of the East in the 8th and 7th centuries B.C. The fact that much Cypriote pottery has been found in the Greek colonies of Tarsus in Asia Minor and Al Mina in Syria may indicate that the Cypriots followed the Greeks in their colonial expansion, or that Cyprus, with its existing Greek cities like Salamis, was used as a stepping-stone, as at the time of the Mycenaean expansion to the East five centuries earlier.

Sanctuaries and Sacred Imagery

The Archaic period is the period of temples and sanctuaries, with statues in limestone and terracotta *(Plates 101, 111, 112)*. Though the evidence for real temples in the Greek sense of the word is very scanty, the sanctuaries are numerous. They usually have a rustic character and the divinity who is worshipped is usually an omnipotent god, combining many different qualities, conceived in the same manner as a saint of the Greek Orthodox religion today. Such gods were mainly fertility gods, since this was the principal problem of an agrarian community. The fertility god, indeed, was the particular god of Cyprus, handed down from prehistoric times. It is chiefly in religion that we see how conservative the Cypriots were and how closely linked with their past, even in the most remote periods.

The sanctuary of Ayia Irini on the north coast, excavated by the Swedish Cyprus Expedition in 1929, had a life of about seven hundred years. It was originally built in the Late Bronze Age (c. 1200 B.C.) and after successive destructions and restorations was finally abandoned c. 500 B.C.[85].

During the last and most important phase in the history of the sanctuary (c. 625–500), it consisted of an enclosure with an altar and a libation table, recalling the Vounous clay model of a sacred enclosure of the Early Bronze Age. About 2000 terracotta figures were found round the altar *(Plate 98)*, representing bull figures, worshippers, war chariots, armed men and centaurs. One of the figures represents a priest wearing a bull's mask. Bulls' masks must have been worn during the ceremonies performed in the Vounous *temenos* in the Early Bronze Age and later at Enkomi, in the two Late Bronze Age sanctuaries where large numbers of skulls of oxen were found on the floors. The two bronze statues of the Enkomi god represent him wearing a horned helmet, an attribute which associates him with fertility. As at Enkomi, where the god soon also became associated with war (as is shown by the second statue), so at Ayia Irini the fertility god of the sanctuary was assigned the functions of a war god, as shown by the terracottas of war chariots and warriors *(Plate 100)*. Some of the latter are life-size.

The workmanship of the terracottas is somewhat crude, but the figures are lively and form attractive groups. The craftsman's sense of humour—a quality which may be often seen in Archaic Cypriote art—is never lacking. The religious importance of the Ayia Irini cult is obvious. It illustrates the most ancient cult of Cyprus, that of the fertility god, which is first seen at Vounous in the Early Bronze Age and developed through the Late Bronze Age at Enkomi and Ayia Irini down to 500 B.C. Something of the soul of Cyprus may be seen in a careful study of the artistic inspiration of the Ayia Irini sanctuary.

Another sanctuary dedicated to a rural god was excavated in 1953 at Meniko near Nicosia[86]. It yielded terracotta figures of good quality, including one of Baal-Hamman seated on a throne *(Plate 103)*, and clay figures of bulls and other animals. The god worshipped in this sanctuary must have been the patron of the farmers and shepherds of the district.

Cyprus in Classical, Hellenistic and Roman Times

The appearance of the Persian Empire as a major power in the Near East affected Cyprus at once, and the island was subdued by the middle of the 6th century. During the whole of the following century Cyprus joined in a panhellenic struggle for freedom, an event which had far reaching political effects. The Greek consciousness of the Cypriots was awakened and closer political and cultural contacts developed between the Greek mainland and Cyprus. It was in this atmosphere that the great king of Salamis, Evagoras I, appeared on the scene of Cypriote politics, as an advocate of the panhellenic ideals of freedom and Greek culture.

Architecture and Politics: the Palace of Vouni

Characteristic of the political and cultural tendencies of the Classical period is the history of the palace of Vouni, built on a plateau on top of a hill near the northern coast, about five miles west of the city of Soloi *(Plates 13, 139)*. It was built in the early years of the 5th century, immediately after the unsuccessful Ionian revolt against the Persians, in which Cyprus also participated. The king of the city of Marion (west of Soloi), a protégé of king Darius, built the palace of Vouni as a fortress to watch over the city of Soloi, known for its pro-Greek tendencies[87]. The original plan of the palace was Oriental (the main apartments being of the tripartite *liwan* type). After the victory of the Athenian general Cimon over the Persians on the soil of Cyprus in 449 B.C. the pro-Persian king of Marion was dethroned and was succeeded by a pro-Greek prince. Apart from its political implications this change also had an effect on the architecture of the palace. Its new occupant very ingeniously changed its character by closing the south-western entrance of the principal room in the royal apartments with a small wall and transferring the entrance to the north-eastern side of the apartments. In doing so, however, he consciously turned the *liwan* type of apartment into a megaron type. The façade of the megaron had a courtyard in front of it, so that the whole character of the building was now changed to resemble the palaces of Mycenaean Greece.

The palace was provided with large store-rooms, kitchens and bathrooms. It also had the oldest sudatorium (sweating room) known in Greek architecture, long before the Romans. Within the precincts of the palace there were also shrines with altars; a sanctuary dedicated to Athena was built on the highest part of the plateau. Among the offerings found here *(Plate 140)* were a terracotta group of Athena mounting a chariot, and a small figure of a cow *(Plate 138)*, probably a copy of the well-known statue by the Greek sculptor Myron. The palace was destroyed by fire c. 380 B.C. The royal family's treasures, including gold bracelets, silver coins, etc., were hidden under the staircase leading to the upper floor, but were not retrieved at the time; they were among the finds made by the Swedish Expedition.

The Vouni palace is one case in which architectural remains are closely connected with political events; this, however, may have been the common pattern of all cultural expressions in the 5th and 4th centuries, a period when the independent kings of the autonomous city states of the island were constantly at war, either against the Persians or with one another.

The Cenotaph of Nicocreon

Another monument which may be connected with political events at the end of the 4th century B.C. is the tumulus near the village of Enkomi *(Plate 154)*, within the necropolis of Salamis, which was excavated by the present writer for the Cyprus Department of Antiquities in 1965 and 1966. The tumulus itself, some 10 m. high and 50 m. in diameter at its base, had repeatedly been tunnelled by peasants and archaeologists, but unsuccessfully, since they were all expecting the tomb to be in the centre of the level area on which the earth was piled up. In our excavations we discovered, well off centre, an exedra of mud bricks measuring 11.50 m. from north to south and 17 m. from east to west *(Plate 155)*. It is about 1 m. high, and has four steps on all four sides. In the middle of the west side is a ramp with vertical side walls built of mud bricks and an internal filling of earth. The surface of the ramp is plastered, as are its side walls. In the centre of the exedra was a conical mound of stones, some burnt by fire, in the form of a regular pyramid, 5.70 m. in diameter at its base and 1.78 m. in height. Having removed the pyramid, except for its base, we found a layer of horizontally arranged mud bricks, encircled by stones which were larger than those on the surface of the pyramid. These mud bricks covered the remains of a large pyre *(Plate 156)*. In addition to the numerous pieces of charcoal and ashes which we found on the thick layer left by this pyre there were also large numbers of objects, including in particular quantities of clay bottles in the shape of alabastra c. 25 cm. high, with external gilding *(Plate 153)*. There were also clay rosettes and miniature pomegranates. Among the metal objects may be mentioned a large number of iron and bronze strips in the form of narrow bands, often decorated with embossed palmettes at one end. These are thought to be arm-bands or the hand grips of shields, the main structure of which would be of leather and wood. Among the small objects were numerous small gilded clay-beads, oval or in the shape of myrtle-fruit, and gilded bronze myrtle leaves, evidently from wreaths. There were also gold rosettes and gold leaves of various sizes. Most of the gold objects, however, had melted in the high temperature of the pyre and were found as numerous drops on the floor of the exedra. Also on the floor, or mixed with charcoal, were numerous carbonised cereals of all kinds and carbonised almonds, grapes and figs *(Plate 152)*.

Of particular importance was the discovery on the pyre of many fragments of statues of unbaked clay, which had evidently hardened in the pyre *(Plate 158)*. These statues were life-size, male and female, and were mould-

121, 122

123

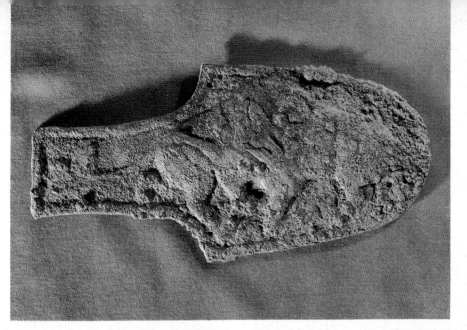

124-126

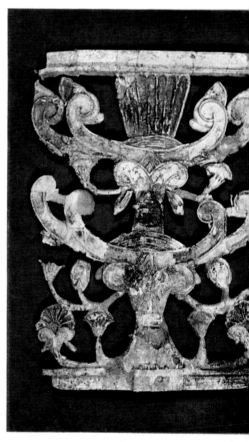

127, 128

129, 130

131, 13.

135

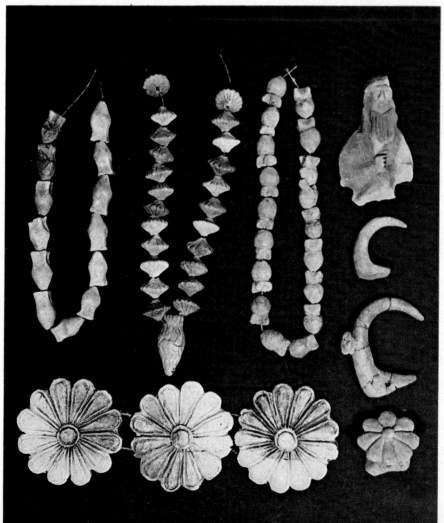

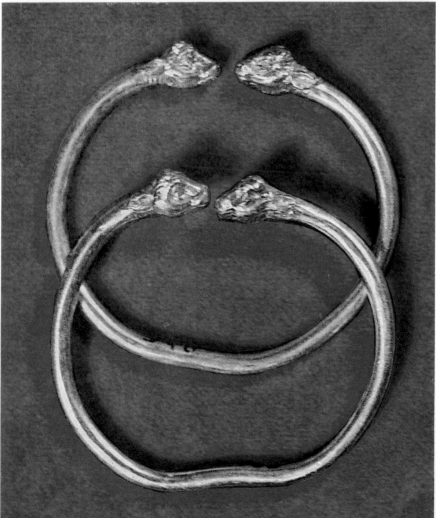

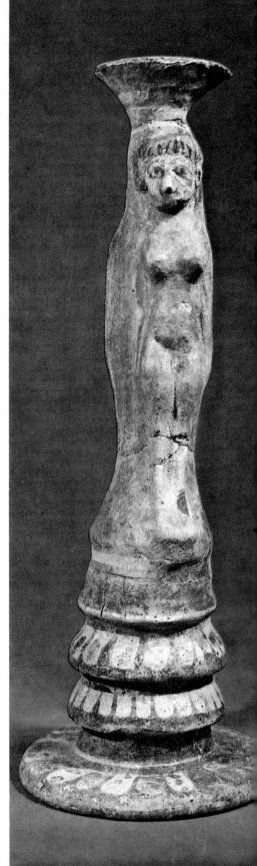

144, 145

146, 147

ed on wooden poles. In many cases large fragments of the statues still preserve the wood or the impression of wood on the back or in the core. The clay was moulded on to iron nails driven into the wooden shaft; in the heads the iron nails were found fixed transversally in the shaft. This explains the presence of hundreds of iron nails on and around the pyre. We are now able to reconstruct part of the funerary ceremony associated with these statues. Sixteen holes were found symmetrically arranged in the exedra, all round the pyre; they were c. 40 cm. deep and contained substantial pieces of carbonised wood. Clearly these holes contained the wooden shafts on which the clay statues were moulded. When the wooden shafts were burnt on the pyre the clay fell off and broke into pieces. Some of the large members (heads, legs, breasts) survived but were often distorted when they fell to the floor. The nails also fell out of the carbonised wood and were scattered. At the end of the ceremony everything was piled in the centre, forming a small mound which was covered with mud bricks and stones. Some of the nails were found round the holes outside the pyramid formed by the pyre. The whole surface of the exedra was affected by the fire, but the heat was particularly intense in the centre, where all the mud bricks turned black.

Five heads of statues have been found, more or less of lifesize. There are two of elderly men, with strong facial characteristics which suggest that they may be of particular people. One of them, with half-open mouth, protruding chin and wavy eyebrows, is undoubtedly a portrait *(Plate 171)*. The other two male heads of younger persons are more or less idealised, as is the only female head *(Plate 158)*. There must have been many more, perhaps sixteen, if we are right in thinking that there was one figure for each of the sixteen holes with the wooden shafts; and in fact there are many more breasts from female figures, legs, arms, etc., all now in fragments which are being restored. Most of them have traces of a red slip on the surface, others are gilded. It is very probable that only those parts of the body which were visible were carefully moulded, the rest of the body being draped. This explains why large pieces (evidently representing torsos) have been found in the form of a *xoanon*, shaped round the wooden shaft, but without any particular shape. The gold or gilt wreaths may have belonged to these figures. In style the heads strongly recall the work of Lysippus. The treatment of the lips, eyes and eyebrows, the intense expression and the particular treatment of the hair date these statues almost precisely to the last quarter of the 4th century. The alabastra and the profusion of gilt objects, both of clay and of iron, point to the same date.

We removed the whole of the material of the pyre, but found no traces of a tomb. The surface of the exedra was absolutely flat. We then removed the whole of the central part of the exedra (leaving only the steps on the four sides) down to the bed-rock without disclosing any traces of a tomb, either burial or incineration. It became evident that this was a cenotaph, consisting of a funerary pyre with offerings and a superimposed tumulus of earth.

There is no doubt that the whole structure was erected in honour of the dead, and that the tumulus was erected at one particular period for a single occasion. The steps of the exedra and the ramp were plastered and never walked on, the pile of stones in the centre of the exedra was covered with mud and never reopened, the tumulus of earth was piled up and never disturbed except by 19th century tomb-robbers. Clearly such a monument must have been associated with a royal funeral.

Since the style of the heads of the statues found on the pyre gives us an almost exact date (the end of the 4th century B.C.) we refer to the history of Salamis and find that the last king of Salamis, Nicocreon, and all the members of the royal family committed suicide and were buried underneath the ruins of the palace. I suggest, though I cannot offer conclusive proof, that the structure just described is a cenotaph in honour of the members of the royal family of Salamis who suffered a tragic death in 311

B.C. It was natural that the death of those who had come to a violent end (βιαιοθάνατοι) should be expiated by fire, either by the Salaminians or by Ptolemy himself; and this would have been a particularly appropriate gesture to an illustrious king. It is possible to go even further and suggest that the statues found on the pyre represent the members of the royal family, the elderly ones in portraits (probably copied from existing representations), the younger ones and the female heads idealised.

Hellenistic Remains

The end of the 4th century marked the end of the Cypriote kingdoms as independent city states, and Cyprus now found itself in the Hellenistic empire under the Ptolemies. It lost the spontaneity of its culture, which now became a provincial offshoot of the homogeneous Hellenistic civilisation. Numerous inscriptions of this period give a clear picture of the new Hellenistic social and cultural institutions of Cyprus, but the purely archaeological evidence is meagre. Of the temples and other public buildings very few traces have survived. No doubt the main reason for this is the continuous occupation of the Hellenistic towns down to the Roman period. The earthquake of A.D. 79 must have destroyed most of the Hellenistic public buildings, and their remains were soon effaced during the large-scale building activities of the Augustan and later Imperial periods. We know of temples at Soloi, where marble friezes with Amazons have been found, and also of a gymnasium at Salamis for which we have epigraphic evidence. But the only monuments of this period now visible are the rock-cut tombs at Nea Paphos, plundered at some time in the past *(Plate 157)*. They have a stepped dromos leading down to a rectangular peristyle courtyard open to the sky with a portico on all four sides which communicates with the funerary chambers. The entablature above the Doric columns is decorated with metopes and triglyphs, all hewn from the rock. This type of tomb may have been introduced from Alexandria, the centre of Ptolemaic culture[88].

The Roman Buildings of Salamis

Numerous imposing buildings of the Roman period have been discovered throughout the island. Soon after Cyprus became a Roman colony in 58 B.C. an earthquake destroyed its late Hellenistic buildings, and thus offered Augustus an opportunity to show his favour towards this new province of the Empire. It was then that some of the most impressive public buildings of Salamis, for example the theatre and the gymnasium, were built.

Though during the Roman period Salamis was no longer the capital of the island, having been replaced by Paphos, it continued nevertheless to be the largest centre in Cyprus, mainly because of the harbour which made it the "Emporium of the East". At the northern extremity of the site the Cyprus Department of Antiquities has been excavating for the last fifteen years, exposing a number of public buildings which must be briefly described[89].

The gymnasium of Salamis *(Plates 169, 170, 173, 174)* was built over the ruins of a Hellenistic gymnasium, of which very few remains have survived, though it is frequently mentioned in inscriptions. The Augustan gymnasium was a simple structure, comprising a range of buildings with a three-sided colonnade along its façade. It was after the earthquakes of A.D. 79 that the plan of the gymnasium was developed, and it was at this time too, under the Emperors Trajan and Hadrian, that it was embellished with marble statues of gods and heroes of Greek mythology *(Plate 174)*. A large four-sided colonnade was built round an open courtyard, measuring 52.50 m. by 39.50 m., with porticos on all four sides. Behind the porticos were rooms, except for the west portico which opened directly into a street through ten doorways. Behind the east portico was an extensive bathing establishment, the rooms of which were decorated with wall mosaics and frescoes in niches *(Plates 173, 175, 176)*. Some of these have been found during the last two years, though badly damaged because the early Christians built up the niches in order to conceal the pagan images. Behind the south-west corner of the palaestra were large and imposing latrines in a semi-circular building *(Plate 170)*.

Severe earthquakes in A.D. 332 and 342 devastated Salamis, along with many other cities on Cyprus. When the gymnasium was rebuilt after some years of abandonment, Salamis was already a Christian city, under the name of Constantia. Only the baths and the palaestra were restored, the latter for use as a meeting-place. Marble columns from the nearby theatre were brought in to replace the broken columns of the colonnade of the palaestra, and marble tiles from the orchestra of the theatre were used for the flooring of the spacious east portico. A number of statues of gods, after being intentionally mutilated, were left in the east portico and the bathrooms for decorative purposes; others were used as building material or were thrown into drains *(Plate 10)*.

With the Arab invasions of the 7th century Salamis received a final blow. By that time its harbour must have been silted up, and its public buildings were now pillaged and burned down. The population fled to the nearby bay of Famagusta, where a new harbour town was built which was destined to become famous in the mediaeval period.

Not far from the gymnasium is the theatre of Salamis *(Plate 8)*, built towards the end of the 1st century B.C. and destroyed in the earthquakes of the 4th century A.D. It had a seating capacity of about 15,000, with a spacious orchestra (27 m. in diameter) and a 40 m. long stage. Though very few of the original rows of seats in the auditorium have survived, it is calculated that originally it may have had more than fifty. The stage building *(frons scenae)* must have been a monumental structure, decorated with marble columns, statues and inscriptions. All this collapsed during the earthquakes of the 4th century, and fragments have been found mixed with débris and stones. The supporting vaults of the auditorium also collapsed, never to be rebuilt *(Plate 7)*. A few squatters built timber huts on and around the thick outer wall of the auditorium. These were burned during the Arab invasions, leaving a thick layer of ashes on the floors, which can be clearly distinguished in the excavated sections.

Epigraphic evidence for an amphitheatre between the theatre and the gymnasium has been proved correct, the amphitheatre having been located but not excavated. Upon its remains a stadium was built in late Roman times.

The excavations in the town centre of Roman Salamis continue year by year, along with repair and reconstruction. It may be hoped that when this complex of four public buildings is finally cleared, a major archaeological area will have been revealed comparable with the best known sites in the Roman East.

The Mosaics of Paphos

Paphos (Nea Paphos) has been in the forefront of archaeological activity during the last three years following the discovery of a large Roman villa of the 3rd century A.D. and well preserved mosaic floors of extremely high quality. The villa, discovered in 1962, is now being excavated by the Cyprus Department of Antiquities[90].

The Roman villa is built on top of ruins of the Hellenistic period. It has more than seventy rooms, arranged round an atrium with a peristyle. On all four sides of the portico, which has a mosaic floor, are rooms, also with mosaic floors. Most of these mosaics represent mythological scenes, usually in panels, with the names of the figures written in Greek letters, for example Pyramus and Thisbe or Icarius and Dionysus *(Plate 178)*. There are also hunting scenes *(Plate 177)* with representations of violent action. The Paphos mosaics are the finest so far discovered on the island.

The bedrooms and bathrooms of the villa are situated along the east side of the atrium, with the kitchens, workshops and other domestic offices extending along the west side. The excavation of the villa has not yet been completed.

Kourion

Large-scale excavations were conducted at Kourion by the Pennsylvania University Museum Expedition from 1934 to 1952. We know from Herodotus that this city was founded by Argive colonists at the end of the Mycenaean period. Remains of this period have in fact been found not far away on Bamboula hill, near the village of Episkopi. We have already referred to the tomb of one of the kings of Kourion of the 11th century B.C., which contained among other objects a gold sceptre with enamel decoration.

Kourion occupied the top of a bluff some 1000 yards long and 500 yards wide, close to the sea and 300 feet above it. Its northern and eastern cliffs were given a steep artificial scarp in a combined operation which served the purposes of both quarrying and defence *(Plate 3)*. The American expedition excavated various public buildings here. These included a theatre[91], probably built in the 2nd century B.C. and remodelled and enlarged during the Roman period. For a short time in the 3rd century A.D. it was used, after modifications required for the safety of the spectators, for the popular spectacle of "hunters fighting with wild animals". The theatre has recently been partially reconstructed and is used for theatrical and musical performances.

The baths, lying east of the theatre, and the palatial building known as the Annexe of Eustolios were built after the destruction of the theatre, and their mosaic floors *(Plates 180, 181)*, were completed early in the 5th century A.D. at a time when Christianity was already established as the official religion. Inscriptions on the mosaic floors refer to the transitional period from paganism to Christianity. One of them specifically mentions Christ; another reminded those who entered the building that it was the abode of Modesty, Temperance and Piety.

The stadium lay outside the limits of the city to the west. It probably had seven rows of seats for some six thousand spectators. It was built in the 2nd century A.D. and remained in use until about A.D. 400. It was partly excavated by the American expedition, and the excavation has recently been completed by the Cyprus Department of Antiquities.

The temple of Apollo Hylates (god of the woodland) lies in a scrub forest *(Plate 179)*, about 1½ miles west of the city site. In antiquity this area was a preserve for deer. The temple started as a small sanctuary in the 8th century B.C. and continued in use until the 4th century A.D. The temple itself, approached by a sacred paved street, had a small cella with a four-columned portico in front of it, reached by a broad flight of steps. In addition to the temple there was a priest's house, a treasury, a palaestra, baths, dormitories for the pilgrims and store-rooms for their votive offerings. The whole area was walled and had two gates for those approaching from Paphos and Kourion respectively. The temple of Apollo was one of the most important in ancient Cyprus, along with the temple of Aphrodite at Paphos and the temple of Zeus at Salamis.

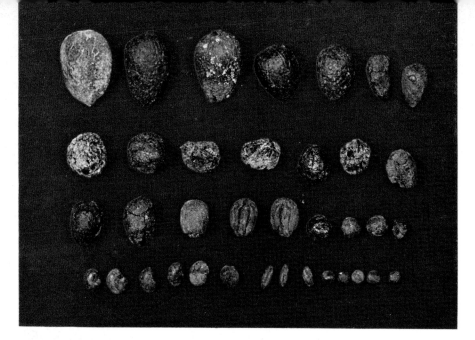

159—163

164, 165

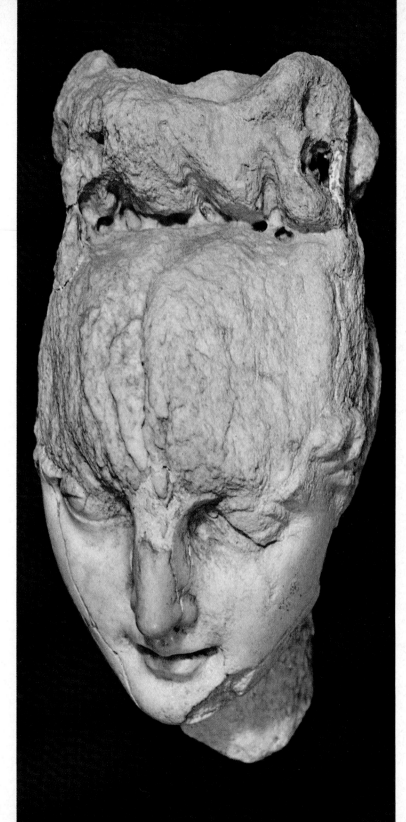

177, 178

EPILOGUE

In describing the most characteristic phases of Cypriote archaeology from the dawn of civilisation on the island down to the end of the Roman period we have confined ourselves to the results obtained during the excavations of recent years. This is not only because these have as a rule been conducted with proper scientific method, but also because in many cases they have corrected the ideas of earlier investigators and given Cypriote archaeology its proper place within the wider archaeological pattern.

To present-day scholarship Cypriote archaeology offers a challenge. In virtue both of its own qualities and of its relations with East and West, the island's ancient culture is no longer considered as provincial and of little interest for its artistic output. Its robust Neolithic culture stands out prominently among the other Neolithic cultures of the Near East. The Early Bronze Age, with its exuberant creative impulses in the field of art, is exceedingly lively and surprisingly progressive. The Late Bronze Age, with its fusion of Aegean and Oriental cultures in Cyprus, gave the island "international" importance. For the first time the Orient made contact with the Occident on Cypriote soil, and the amalgamation of the two had beneficial effects on both, producing results which influenced later historical and artistic developments in the Eastern Mediterranean. The finds in the Geometric and Archaic tombs of Salamis demonstrate the quality of the island's culture and allow us to estimate the decisive role played by Cyprus in the contact between East and West and the creation of the orientalising style in the Aegean area.

The individuality of Cypriote culture diminished somewhat in the classical period, though the Vouni palace and the cenotaph of Nicocreon, described above, offer us insights into the island's glorious past.

During the Hellenistic and Roman periods Cyprus was merely an element in larger empires, with no distinctive character of its own. No doubt remains of impressive public buildings are still waiting to be found in addition to those which recent excavations have revealed. Our picture of the wealth of Salamis, of its harbour, and of the glamour which Paphos drew from the cult of Aphrodite is likely to be filled out by the discovery of further remains of their material culture.

The earthquakes of the 4th century were a disaster to the ancient cities of Cyprus. They must have dislocated their water supplies—as we can see, for example, at Kourion—and may thus have hastened their abandonment. At Salamis the aqueduct which brought water from Kythrea, some thirty miles inland, had been destroyed but was repaired when the city was rebuilt during the early Christian period *(Plate 168)*. But the final catastrophe befell the ancient cities of the island in the 7th century, as a result of the Arab invasions. Thus ended an ancient splendour which had endured six thousand five hundred years. The Cypriots were conscious of this glorious past. When the Salaminians commemorated the deeds of a high official during the last years of the city's life, they boasted that "with his pious laws and good administration he revived for Cyprus its pristine glory". But no doubt these were already empty words. The end was approaching.

NOTES

[1] For references to Cyprus by mediaeval and later travellers see C.D. Cobham, *Excerpta Cypria* (Cambridge, 1908) and T. Mogabgab, *Supplementary Excerpts on Cyprus*, I–III (Nicosia, 1941–1945).

[2] Mogabgab, *op. cit.*, III, 149.

[3] O. Masson gives a detailed account of the interest of 19th century scholars in the Cypriote syllabic script, and traces the history of its decipherment *(Les Inscriptions Chypriotes Syllabiques* (Etudes Chypriotes I), Paris, 1961), 18 ff.

[4] Cesnola described his operations in a book entitled *Cyprus, its Ancient Cities, Tombs and Temples* (London, 1877).

[5] In addition to a number of articles which appeared in periodicals and newspapers of the period, M. Ohnefalsch-Richter attempted a study of Cypriote archaeology in his book *Kypros, the Bible and Homer* (London, 1888).

[6] This British Museum expedition summarised the results of its excavations in *Excavations in Cyprus* (London, 1900).

[7] Myres' contribution to Cypriote archaeology may be found in two of his books, *Handbook of the Cesnola Collection of Antiquities from Cyprus (The Metropolitan Museum of Art)* (New York, 1914) and (in collaboration with M. Ohnefalsch-Richter) *A Catalogue of the Cyprus Museum* (Oxford, 1899).

[8] E. Gjerstad had already visited Cyprus in 1924 and studied the prehistory of the island. His book *Studies on Prehistoric Cyprus* (Uppsala, 1926) is of fundamental importance.

[9] The Swedish Cyprus Expedition published three large volumes (in two parts, text and plates) describing the results of the excavations: *The Swedish Cyprus Expedition, Finds and Results of the Excavations in Cyprus, 1927–1931* (Stockholm, 1934, 1935, 1937). Volumes of synthesis, describing the archaeology of Cyprus from the Neolithic period down to the Roman period, have also appeared. Reference to these is made below.

[10] C.F.A. Schaeffer excavated in the Early Bronze Age necropolis at Vounous, but his pioneer work is connected with the study of the Late Bronze Age in Cyprus. His excavations at Enkomi constitute a landmark in the study of Cypriote archaeology. In his *Missions en Chypre 1932–1935* (Paris, 1936) he discusses problems of prehistoric Cyprus, while in his *Enkomi-Alasia*, I (Paris, 1952) he describes in detail the results of his first excavation campaigns at Enkomi. At the time of writing he is continuing his excavations at Enkomi every year.

[11] P. Dikaios, associated with the Cyprus Museum (as Curator) and later with the Department of Antiquities (as Director) for some thirty years, did pioneer work in the study of the Neolithic period with his excavations at Khirokitia, Erimi and Sotira (all published). In his "The Stone Age in Cyprus" (first part of *The Swedish Cyprus Expedition*, IV (IA), Lund, 1961) he wrote a general survey of the Neolithic culture of Cyprus. He also excavated at the Early Bronze Age cemetery of Vounous and published the results of his excavations in *Archaeologia*, 88 (1938); his latest excavation at Enkomi (jointly with Professor Schaeffer) has thrown new light on the Late Bronze Age period; he is now working on the publication of the results.

[12] Various Swedish scholars have dealt with specific periods of Cypriote archaeology. We have already mentioned Gjerstad's *Studies on Prehistoric Cyprus*. His monumental work on Iron Age, Archaic and Classical Cyprus *(The Swedish Cyprus Expedition* IV (2), Stockholm, 1948), will remain for the foreseeable future the standard work on these periods. E. Sjöqvist, a member of the Swedish Cyprus Expedition, dealt with the Late Bronze Age period *(Problems of the Late Cypriote Bronze Age*, Stockholm, 1941), and P. Åström with the Middle Bronze

Age (*The Middle Cypriote Bronze Age*, Lund, 1957). The Australian scholar James R. Stewart has given us a monumental work on the Early Bronze Age period, first with his *Vounous 1937– 1938* (Lund, 1950) and then with his contribution in *The Swedish Cyprus Expedition*, IV (IA) on the Early Bronze Age period in Cyprus in general. Equally important contributions on specific periods made by other scholars are mentioned elsewhere in this book.

[13] For a study of this problem see H.W. Catling, *Cyprus in the Neolithic and Bronze Age Periods* (*Cambridge Ancient History*, revised edition of Vols. I–II), 7.

[14] For a recent study of craniological problems in Neolithic Cyprus see R.-P. Charles, *Le peuplement de Chypre dans l'antiquité* (Etudes Chypriotes, II, Paris, 1962), 59 ff.

[15] The first campaign of excavation was carried out in 1965 under the direction of Dr T. Watkins, sponsored by the University of Birmingham. See first preliminary report in *Bulletin de Correspondance Hellénique*, 90 (1966), 358 ff.

[16] Cf. P. Dikaios, *The Swedish Cyprus Expedition*, IV (IA), 190.

[17] Cf. J.R. Stewart, *ibid.*, 269 f.

[18] Cf. H.W. Catling, *op. cit.*, 26.

[19] For relations between Crete and Cyprus in prehistoric times see H.W. Catling and V. Karageorghis, "Minoica in Cyprus", *Annual of the British School at Athens*, 55 (1960), 109 ff.

[20] Cf. Catling, *op. cit.*, 43 ff., for a general discussion of the relations of Cyprus with her neighbours during the Middle Bronze Age.

[21] For recent expressions of contrary views, see H.W. Catling in *Annual of the British School at Athens*, 60 (1965), 212 ff., and V. Karageorghis, *Nouveaux Documents pour l'Etude du Bronze Récent à Chypre* (Etudes Chypriotes III, Paris, (1965), 201 ff.

[22] On problems connected with the origin of the Cypro-Minoan script see Masson, *op. cit.*, 34 ff.

[23] Cf. Catling, *Cyprus in the Neolithic and Bronze Age Periods*, 65.

[24] Cf. *ibid.*, 58 ff.

[25] For a recent discussion of this problem see J. Pouilloux, in *Comptes Rendus de l'Académie des Inscriptions et Belles Lettres*, 1966, 248, 254.

[26] Preliminary reports on the excavations at Kition have appeared in the *Bulletin de Correspondance Hellénique* every year since 1963.

[27] Cf. Catling, *ibid.*, 72 f.

[28] Cf. J. Deshayes, *La Nécropole de Ktima* (Paris, 1963), 9 ff.

[29] This may perhaps be the motive which made Aeschylus speak about a "Cypriote character" in one of his tragedies. This passage, however, has not always been interpreted without bias by some modern historians, who have seen—erroneously—a desire on the part of Aeschylus to differentiate ethnically and politically between the Greeks of Cyprus and the Greeks of the mainland. (Cf. Sir George Hill, A *History of Cyprus*, I, 94).

[30] The new Antiquities Law of 1964 declares that all antiquities found during excavations are the property of the State.

[31] For a discussion of this subject see O. Masson in *Bulletin de Correspondance Hellénique*, 89 (1964), 213 ff.

[32] D.G. Hogarth, *Devia Cypria, Notes on an Archaeological Journey in Cyprus in 1888* (London, 1889).

[33] See discussion by the present writer in *Bulletin de Correspondance Hellénique*, 89 (1964), 266 f.

[34] See discussion by the present writer in *Antiquity*, 1966, 45 ff.

[35] See description by the present writer in *Bulletin de Correspondance Hellénique*, 89 (1964), 268 ff.

[36] For both these instances see *Archäologischer Anzeiger*, 1963, 547 ff., and 1966, 233 ff., 242 ff., respectively.

[37] See George McFadden in *American Journal of Archaeology*, 58 (1954), 131 ff.

[38] See Schaeffer, *Enkomi-Alasia*, I, 10 (note by René Dussaud).

[39] Some of the results of this survey have been incorporated by Catling in his article "Patterns of Settlement in Bronze Age Cyprus", *Opuscula Atheniensia*, IV (1963), 129 ff.

[40] See description by the present writer in *Bulletin de Correspondance Hellénique*, 84 (1960), 504 ff.

[41] See details about these discoveries by the present writer in *Bulletin de Correspondance Hellénique*, 91 (1967), 337 ff.

[42] This material is now being studied by Professor R.-P. Charles, whose report will appear as an appendix in the final publication of the necropolis.

[43] The material has already been studied by Dr P. Ducos of the Institut de Paléontologie of Paris.

[44] *American Journal of Archaeology*, 65 (1961), 305.

[45] Cf. note 21.

[46] See H.J. Appel, "Elektronische Steuerung einer chemischen Anlage", *Archaeo-Physica, Beihefte der Bonner Jahrbücher*, 15 (1965). The method is now practised in the Rheinisches Landesmuseum, Bonn.

[47] For the methods employed during cleaning see technical report by Dr Plenderleith in Schaeffer's *Enkomi-Alasia*, I, 381 ff.

[48] Cf. P. Dikaios, *A Guide to the Cyprus Museum* (3rd ed., 1961).

[49] See P. Dikaios in *The Swedish Cyprus Expedition*, IV (IA), 2.

[50] This new evidence is published by L. Kahil and the present writer in *Antike Kunst*, 1967, 133 ff.

[51] The results of the excavations have been published by P. Dikaios in *Khirokitia* (Oxford, 1953).

[52] P. Dikaios, in *The Swedish Cyprus Expedition*, IV (IA), 106 ff.

[53] *Idem.*, *Sotira* (Philadelphia, 1961).

[54] *Idem.*, "The excavations at Erimi, 1933–1935, Final Report", *Report of the Department of Antiquities of Cyprus 1936* (Nicosia 1938), 1–81.

[55] See *Bulletin de Correspondance Hellénique*, 84 (1960), 244 ff.

[56] See Gjerstad, *Studies on Prehistoric Cyprus*, 19 ff.; P. Dikaios, "A Conspectus of Architecture in Ancient Cyprus", *Kypriakai Spoudai*, 24 (1960), 7 f.

[57] Cf. notes 16–17.

[58] Cf. O. Masson, *Les Inscriptions Chypriotes Syllabiques*, 34.

[59] P. Åström, *The Middle Cypriote Bronze Age*, 1 ff.

[60] Catling, *Cyprus in the Neolithic and Bronze Age Periods*, 38.

[61] J.R. Stewart, "The Tomb of the Seafarer at Karmi in Cyprus", *Opuscula Atheniensia*, IV (1963), 197 ff.

[62] Lavishly illustrated by Rafael Larco Hoyle, *Peru* (Archaeologia Mundi, 1966).

[63] Catling and Karageorghis, "Minoika in Cyprus", *Annual of the British School at Athens*, 55 (1960), 109 ff.

[64] M. Popham, "Two Cypriot Sherds from Crete", *Annual of the British School at Athens*, 58 (1963), 89 ff.

[65] Inadequately published by Murray and others, *Excavations in Cyprus* (London, 1900), 1–54.

[66] *The Swedish Cyprus Expedition*, I, 467 ff.

[67] We have already referred to the first volume of *Enkomi-Alasia*, I (Paris, 1952); the second volume is in preparation.

[68] This problem is discussed by the present writer in *Nouveaux Documents pour l'Etude du Bronze Récent à Chypre* (Paris, 1965), 201 ff.

[69] See discussion by the present writer in *American Journal of Archaeology*, 62 (1958), 383 ff.

[70] See *Nouveaux Documents pour l'Etude du Bronze Récent à Chypre*, 231 ff.

[71] Schaeffer, *Enkomi-Alasia*, I, 379 ff.

[72] Cf. discussion by the present writer in *Kypriakai Spoudai*, 25 (1961), 7 ff.

[73] P. Dikaios, "The Bronze Statue of a Horned God from Enkomi", *Archäologischer Anzeiger*, 1962, 1 ff.

[74] C.F.A. Schaeffer, "Götter der Nord- und Inselvölker in Cypern", *Archiv für Orientforschung*, XXI (1965), 59 ff.

[75] Cf. Helene Kantor, "Syro-Palestinian Ivories", *Journal of Near Eastern Studies*, XV (1956), 171, for commentary and references.

[76] Cf. *Bulletin de Correspondance Hellénique*, 90 (1966), 346 ff.

[77] Cf. preliminary reports by the present writer in *Bulletin de Correspondance Hellénique*, 84 (1960), 504 ff., and in the same periodical from 1963 to date.

[78] For a discussion of this chronological problem see Catling "A Bronze Greave from a 13th century B.C. Tomb at Enkomi", *Opuscula Atheniensia*, II (1955), 21 ff.

[79] J. du Plat Taylor and others, *Myrtou-Pigadhes: A Late Bronze Age Sanctuary in Cyprus* (Oxford, 1957).

[80] See note 37.

[81] For reports about Salamis see *Bulletin de Correspondance Hellénique* since 1963 and *Archäologischer Anzeiger*, 1966.

[82] See note 25.

[83] Published by P. Dikaios in *Archäologischer Anzeiger*, 1963, 126 ff.

[84] Cf. *Bulletin de Correspondance Hellénique*, 87 (1963), 292 ff.

[85] For a discussion of the cult of the Ayia Irini sanctuary see E. Sjöqvist, "Die Kultgeschichte eines cyprischen Temenos", *Archiv für Religionswissenschaft* (1933), 308 ff.

[86] See *Archäologischer Anzeiger*, 1963, 559 f.

[87] The architecture of the Palace of Vouni is described in *The Swedish Cyprus Expedition*, vol. III, 111 ff. For the history of the palace see also *The Swedish Cyprus Expedition*, IV (2), 488 ff.

[88] On Hellenistic architecture in Cyprus see *The Swedish Cyprus Expedition*, IV (3), 1 ff.

[89] Two volumes describing the sculptures found in the excavations of Salamis have already been published: *Sculptures from Salamis* I and II (1964, 1966), with brief descriptions of the principal monuments of Salamis revealed during recent excavations.

[90] For brief preliminary reports see *Bulletin de Correspondance Hellénique* since 1963.

[91] The architecture of the theatre has recently been published by R. Stillwell, "Kourion— the Theater", *Proceedings of the American Philosophical Society*, 105 (1961). Other reports on the excavations at Kourion appeared in the *University Museum of Pennsylvania Bulletin*, 1935– 1952, and the *American Journal of Archaeology*, 50 (1946), 449 ff.

CHRONOLOGY*

Period		B.C. (approx.)	Associations
Neolithic	IA:	5800–5250	
	IB:	5250–4950	
	II:	3500–3000	
Chalcolithic	I:	3000–2500	
	II:	2500–2300	
Early Bronze Age or Early Cypriote	I:	2300–2200	
	II:	2200–2100	
	III:	2100–2000	
Middle Bronze Age or Middle Cypriote	:	2000–1600	Hyksos, end of 17th century
Late Bronze Age or Late Cypriote	IA:	1600–1450	
	IB:	1450–1400	
	IIA:	1400–1300	Mycenaean trade expansion. Appearance of Mycenaean pottery in large quantities
	IIB:	1300–1230	
	IIIA:	1230–1190	Achaean colonisation
	IIIB:	1190–1150	The Peoples of the Sea
	IIIC:	1150–1050	Destruction by earthquakes of Late Bronze Age cities
Cypro-Geometric	I:	1050–950	
	II:	950–850	
	III:	850–700	709 B.C.–569 B.C.: Assyrian domination
Cypro-Archaic	I:	700–600	569 B.C.–546 B.C.: Egyptian domination
	II:	600–475	546 B.C.–332 B.C.: Persian domination 499/8: Revolt of Onesilos against the Persians
Cypro-Classical	I:	475–400	411 B.C.–374 B.C.: King Evagoras I of Salamis
	II:	400–325	
Hellenistic	I:	325–150	332 B.C.–323 B.C.: Cyprus freed by Alexander the Great
	II:	150–50	294 B.C.–58 B.C.: Ptolemaic period
Roman	I:	50 B.C.–A.D.150	58 B.C.–A.D. 330: Roman period
	II:	A.D.150–A.D.250	A.D. 45, conversion to Christianity by SS. Paul and Barnabas
	III:	From about A.D. 250	

* This chronology is based mainly on that given in P. Dikaios, *A Guide to the Cyprus Museum* (3rd edit. 1961) and *The Swedish Cyprus Expedition* vols. IV (2) and IV (3), except for the Late Bronze Age chronology, which is based on recent research.

THE MAIN EXCAVATIONS

Period	Site	Location
Neolithic IA	Petra tou Limniti	Small island off the north-western coast
Neolithic IA	Khirokitia	Larnaca district, 4 miles inland from south coast
Neolithic IB	Troulli	North coast, 10 miles east of Kyrenia
Neolithic II	Kalavassos A	4 miles south-west of Khirokitia
Neolithic II	Sotira	Limassol district, 4 miles north-west of Kourion
Chalcolithic I	Kalavassos B	A short distance north of Kalavassos A
Chalcolithic I	Erimi	8 miles west of Limassol
Chalcolithic II	Ambelikou	Near the north coast, Nicosia district, 4 miles north of Soloi
Chalcolithic II	Philia-Drakos	Nicosia district, c. 15 miles west of Nicosia
Early Cypriote I	Philia B	*do.*
Early Cypriote I	Vasilia	Kyrenia district, c. 12 miles west of Kyrenia, near the north coast
Early Cypriote II	Vounous A	Kyrenia district, c. 5 miles south-east of Kyrenia
Early Cypriote III	Vounous B	*do.*
Early Cypriote III	Episkopi (Phaneromeni)	Limassol district, c. 10 miles west of Limassol
Middle Cypriote	Kalopsidha	Famagusta district, west of Famagusta
Middle Cypriote	Kalopsidha	*do.*
Middle Cypriote	Karmi	Kyrenia district, c. 5 miles south-west of Kyrenia
Late Cypriote	Enkomi	Famagusta district, c. 5 miles north-west of Famagusta, near the east coast
Late Cypriote	Enkomi	*do.*

IN CYPRUS IN RECENT YEARS

Directing Staff	Date	Publication
E. Gjerstad (Swedish Cyprus Expedition)	1927-1931	*The Swedish Cyprus Expedition* (hereafter *SCE*) I
P. Dikaios (Cyprus Museum and Department of Antiquities)	1936-1939 and 1946	*Khirokitia* (Oxford, 1953)
P. Dikaios (Department of Antiquities)	1941	*SCE* IV (IA), 63 ff.
do	1947	*Ibid.*, 106 ff.
P. Dikaios (for Pennsylvania University Museum, Philadelphia)	1947, 1951-2, 1954, 1956	P. Dikaios, *Sotira* (Philadelphia, 1961)
P. Dikaios (Department of Antiquities)	1947	*SCE* IV (IA), 133 ff.
P. Dikaios (Department of Antiquities)	1933, 1935	*Report of the Department of Antiquities*, 1936-I, *SCE* IV (IA), 113 ff.
do	1942, 1953	*SCE* IV (IA), 141 ff.
T. Watkins (Birmingham University)	1965	Unpublished
P. Dikaios (Department of Antiquities)	1943	*SCE* IV (IA), 150 ff.
J.R. Stewart (Melbourne Cyprus Expedition)	1955	Unpublished
E. and J. Stewart (British School at Athens)	1937-1938	E. and J. Stewart, *Vounous 1937–38* (Lund, 1950)
P. Dikaios, C.F.A. Schaeffer (Cyprus Museum and Louvre Museum Excavations)	1931-1933	P. Dikaios, "The Excavations at Vounous Bellapais, 1931-32", *Archaeologia* 88 (1938), 1-174; C.F.A. Schaeffer, *Missions en Chypre 1932–1935* (Paris, 1936)
S. Weinberg (University of Missouri)	1955	*Archaeology* 9 (1956), 112 ff.
E. Gjerstad	1924	E. Gjerstad, *Studies on Prehistoric Cyprus*, 27 ff.
P. Åström	1960	*Excavations at Kalopsidha and Ayios Iakovos in Cyprus* (Lund, 1966).
J.R. Stewart (Melbourne Cyprus Expedition)	1962	Unpublished
E. Sjöqvist (Swedish Cyprus Expedition)	1929	*SCE* I, 302 ff.
C.F.A. Schaeffer (Centre National de la Recherche Scientifique) and P. Dikaios (Department of Antiquities	1934, 1946 to present day.	C.F.A. Schaeffer, *Enkomi-Alasia* I (Paris, 1952)

Period	Site	Location
Late Cypriote	Myrtou-Pigadhes	Kyrenia district, c. 20 miles south-west of Kyrenia, 5 miles from the north coast
Middle Cypriote and Late Cypriote	Myrtou-Stephania	*do.*
Late Cypriote	Kition	Larnaca district (modern Lanaca)
Late Cypriote	Sinda	Famagusta district, c. 10 miles west of Enkomi
Late Cypriote	Palaeokastro-Maa	Paphos district, c. 6 miles north of Ktima, on the coast
Late Cypriote	Pyla-Kokkinokremnos	Larnaca district, c. 7 miles north-east of Larnaca.
Late Cypriote and later	Kouklia	Paphos district, c. 10 miles south-east of Ktima
Late Cypriote to Early Iron Age and later	Salamis (south sector)	Famagusta district, c. 5 miles north of Famagusta, on the coast
Late Cypriote and Early Iron Age	Kourion (Bamboula and Kaloriziki)	Limassol district, c. 10 miles west of Limassol, near the south coast
Geometric to Archaic	Salamis (necropolis)	Famagusta district
Geometric to Archaic	Ktima	Paphos district, west coast
Archaic	Ayia Irini	Kyrenia district north-western coast
Archaic to Roman and Early Christian	Kourion (city site, Sanctuary of Apollo and Ay. Ermogenis necropolis)	Limassol district, south coast
Archaic to Roman and Early Christian	Soloi	Nicosia district, north coast, in Morphou Bay
Archaic to Roman	Kouklia	Paphos district

Directing Staff	Date	Publication
J. du Plat Taylor and others (Ashmolean Museum, Oxford, and University of Sydney)	1950-51	J. du Plat Taylor and others, *Myrtou-Pigadhes* (Oxford, 1957)
do.	1951	J.B. Hennessy, *Stephania: a Middle and Late Bronze Age Cemetery in Cyprus* (London, 1965)
V. Karageorghis (Dept. of Antiquities)	1959, 1962 to present day	Preliminary Reports in *Bulletin de Correspondance Hellénique* since 1959.
A. Furumark (University of Uppsala)	1947-1948	*Opuscula Atheniensia* VI (1965), 99 ff.
P. Dikaios (Department of Antiquities)	1954	Unpublished
P. Dikaios (Department of Antiquities)	1952	Unpublished
Mitford, Iliffe and others (University of St Andrews and Liverpool Museums)	1951-1953	Unpublished
J. Pouilloux and others (Institut F. Courby, University of Lyons)	1964 to present day	Unpublished
J.F. Daniel, G. McFadden (Pennsylvania University Museum)	1934-1939	J.F. Daniel, *American Journal of Archaeology* 41 (1937), 56 ff. G. McFadden, *American Journal of Archaeology* 58 (1954), 131 ff.
P. Dikaios, V. Karageorghis (Dept. of Antiquities)	P. Dikaios 1957, Karageorghis 1962 to present day.	P. Dikaios in *Archäologischer Anzeiger* 1963 and V. Karageorghis in *Bulletin de Correspondance Hellénique* since 1962
J. Bérard, J. Deshayes	1935-1955	J. Deshayes, *La Nécropole de Ktima* (Paris, 1963).
E. Gjerstad (Swedish Cyprus Expedition)	1929	*SCE* II, 642 ff.
B. Hill, R. Young, J. Young, G. McFadden, J.S. Last	1934-1952	Preliminary reports in *University Museum of Pennsylvania Bulletin*, 1935-1950. *American Journal of Archaeology* 50 (1946), 449 ff. Final report on theatre by Stillwell in *Proceedings of the American Philosophical Society* 105 (1961)
J. des Gagniers, T. Thin, L. Kahil, R. Ginouvès (Université Laval, Quebec)	1964 to present day	Unpublished
G.F. Maier and others (Deutsches Archäologisches Institut, Berlin)	1966	Unpublished

Period	Site	Location
Classical	Vouni	Nicosia district, north coast, north-west of Soloi
Hellenistic	Kato Paphos	Paphos district, south-west coast
Roman	Soloi	Nicosia district, north coast
Roman	Kato Paphos	Paphos district, south-west coast
Roman	Kourion (stadium)	Limassol district
Roman	Salamis (north sector)	Famagusta district, on east coast

Directing Staff	Date	Publication
E. Gjerstad (Swedish Cyprus Expedition)	1928-1929	*SCE* III, 76 ff.
K. Michalowski and others (Warsaw University)	1965 to present day	Unpublished
E. Gjerstad (Swedish Cyprus Expedition)	1929	*SCE* III, 399 ff.
K. Nicolaou (Dept. of Antiquities)	1962 to present day	Preliminary report in *Report of the Department of Antiquities, Cyprus,* 1963
J. Young (Pennsylvania University Museum) and J.S. Last (Department of Antiquities)	J. Young 1933, J.S. Last 1964-1966	Unpublished
V. Karageorghis and A.I. Dikigoropoulos	V. Karageorghis and A.I. Dikigoropoulos 1952-1959, V. Karageorghis 1959 to present day	Preliminary reports in *Journal of Hellenic Studies* (Archaeology in Cyprus), in *Bulletin de Correspondance Hellénique* (1958-1966), V. Karageorghis and C.C. Vermeule *Sculptures from Salamis* I-II (1964-1966)

Note This table refers to excavations the results of which are mentioned directly or indirectly in this book. The author does not consider those excavations which are not mentioned here to be of minor importance, but they are omitted as outside the scope of a book addressed to the general public. Recent excavations about which only very short preliminary reports have so far appeared are considered here as unpublished unless otherwise stated.

BIBLIOGRAPHY

A. General

CASSON, S.: *Ancient Cyprus* (London, 1937).

CHARLES, R.-P.: *Le peuplement de Chypre dans l'antiquité. Etude anthropologique* (Etudes Chypriotes, II, Paris, 1962).

DIKAIOS, P.: "A Conspectus of Architecture in Ancient Cyprus", *Kypriakai Spoudai*, 24 (1960).

DIKAIOS, P.: *A Guide to the Cyprus Museum* (3rd ed., Nicosia, 1961).

GJERSTAD, E., and others: *The Swedish Cyprus Expedition. Finds and Results of the Excavations in Cyprus 1927–1931*, I–III (Stockholm, 1934–1937).

HILL, Sir George F.: *A History of Cyprus*, I (Cambridge, 1940).

KARAGEORGHIS, V.: *Treasures in the Cyprus Museum* (Nicosia, 1962).

KARAGEORGHIS, V.: "Ten Years of Archaeology in Cyprus, 1953–1962", *Archäologischer Anzeiger*, 1963.

KARAGEORGHIS, V.: "Chronique des fouilles et découvertes archéologiques à Chypre" (yearly report on archaeology in Cyprus from 1958 to date, in *Bulletin de Correspondance Hellénique*).

B. Neolithic

CATLING, H.W.: *Cyprus in the Neolithic and Bronze Age Periods* (Cambridge Ancient History, revised edition of Volumes I and II, Cambridge, 1966).

DIKAIOS, P.: *Khirokitia* (Oxford, 1953).

DIKAIOS, P.: *Sotira* (Philadelphia, 1961).

DIKAIOS, P., and STEWART, J.R.: *The Swedish Cyprus Expedition*, vol. IV (IA). *The Stone Age and the Bronze Age in Cyprus* (Lund, 1962).

GJERSTAD, E.: *Studies on Prehistoric Cyprus* (Uppsala, 1926).

SCHAEFFER, C.F.A.: *Missions en Chypre, 1932–1935* (Paris, 1936).

C. Early and Middle Bronze Age

ÅSTRÖM, P.: *The Middle Cypriote Bronze Age* (Lund, 1957).

CATLING, H.W.: *Cyprus in the Neolithic and Bronze Age Periods* (Cambridge Ancient History, revised edition of Volumes I and II, Cambridge, 1966).

DIKAIOS, P.: "The Excavations at Vounous-Bellapais in Cyprus, 1931–1932", *Archaeologia*, 88 (1938), 1–174.

DIKAIOS, P., and STEWART, J.R.: *The Swedish Cyprus Expedition*, vol. IV (IA). *The Stone Age and the Bronze Age in Cyprus* (Lund, 1962).

GJERSTAD, E.: *Studies on Prehistoric Cyprus* (Uppsala, 1926).

HENNESSY, J.B.: *Stephania: A Middle and Late Bronze Age Cemetery in Cyprus* (London, *n.d.*).

SCHAEFFER, C.F.A.: *Missions en Chypre, 1932–1935* (Paris, 1936).

STEWART, E., and STEWART, J.R.: *Vounous, 1937–1938* (Lund, 1950).

D. Late Bronze Age

ÅSTRÖM, Lena: *Studies on the Arts and Crafts of the Late Cypriote Bronze Age* (Lund, 1967).

CATLING, H.W.: *Cypriote Bronzework in the Mycenaean World* (Oxford, 1964).

CATLING, H.W.: *Cyprus in the Neolithic and Bronze Age Periods* (Cambridge Ancient History, revised edition of Volumes I and II, Cambridge, 1966).

DESBOROUGH, V.R. d'A.: *The Last Mycenaeans and their Successors* (Oxford, 1964).

TAYLOR, J. du Plat, and others: *Myrtou-Pigadhes: A Late Bronze Age Sanctuary in Cyprus* (Oxford, 1957).

FURUMARK, A.: *The Mycenaean Pottery, Analysis and Classification* (Stockholm, 1941).

GJERSTAD, E.: *Studies on Prehistoric Cyprus* (Uppsala, 1926).

HENNESSY, J.B.: *Stephania: A Middle and Late Bronze Age Cemetery in Cyprus* (London, *n.d.*).

KARAGEORGHIS, V.: *Corpus Vasorum Antiquorum, Cyprus*, I (1963), II (1965).

KARAGEORGHIS, V.: *Nouveaux Documents pour l'Etude du Bronze Récent à Chypre* (Etudes Chypriotes, III, Paris, 1965).

SCHAEFFER, C.F.A.: *Missions en Chypre, 1932–1935* (Paris, 1936).

SCHAEFFER, C.F.A.: *Enkomi-Alasia*, I (Paris, 1952).

SJÖQVIST, E.: *Problems of the Late Cypriote Bronze Age* (Stockholm, 1940).

STUBBINGS, F.H.: *Mycenaean Pottery from the Levant* (Cambridge, 1951).

E. Iron Age to Classical

BOARDMAN, J.: *The Greeks Overseas* (London, 1964).

DESHAYES, J.: *La Nécropole de Ktima: Mission Jean Bérard 1953–1955* (Paris, 1963).

GJERSTAD, E.: *The Swedish Cyprus Expedition*, IV (2). *The Cypro-Geometric, Cypro-Archaic and Cypro-Classical Periods* (Stockholm, 1948).

KARAGEORGHIS, V.: "Recent Discoveries at Salamis (Cyprus)", *Archäologischer Anzeiger*, 1966.

MASSON, O.: *Inscriptions Chypriotes Syllabiques. Recueil Critique et Commenté.* (Etudes Chypriotes, I, Paris, 1961).

SPYRIDAKIS, K.: Κύπριοι Βαδιλεῖς του 4ου αἰ. π.Χ. (411–311/10 π.Χ.).

E. Hellenistic and Roman

KARAGEORGHIS, V.: *Sculptures from Salamis*, I (Nicosia, 1964).

KARAGEORGHIS, V., and VERMEULE, C.C.: *Sculptures from Salamis*, II, (Nicosia, 1966).

STILLWELL, R.: "Kourion—the Theater", *Proceedings of the American Philosophical Society* 105, 1, Feb. 1961.

VESSBERG, O., and WESTHOLM, A.: *The Swedish Cyprus Expedition*, vol. IV (3). *The Hellenistic and Roman Periods in Cyprus* (Stockholm, 1956).

LIST OF ILLUSTRATIONS

1 *Remains of the sea-tower of Amathus.*
2 *The unexcavated acropolis of Amathus, from the south.*
3 *The fortified hill of Kourion, from the east.*
4 *Salamis, the gymnasium: north and west stoas before excavation.*
5 *Salamis, the gymnasium: west and north stoas before excavation.*
6 *The shore at the city site of Salamis, looking south towards the harbour. A forest of mimosas covers the ruins of the city.*
7 *Salamis, the theatre: part of a wall which collapsed during the earthquakes of the 4th century A.D.*
8 *Salamis, the theatre: in the background an unexcavated amphitheatre (left) and the columns of the gymnasium (right).*
9 *General view of the Neolithic settlement of Troulli.*
10 *Salamis, the gymnasium: marble sculptures in one of the swimming pools of the baths, as found during the recent excavations.*
11 *The hill occupied by the Neolithic settlement of Khirokitia, from the south-west.*
12 *Detail of the Neolithic settlement of Khirokitia, from the north. In the background the River Maroniou.*
13 *The courtyard of the megaron of the Vouni palace. In the background the small island of Petra tou Limniti (top right).*
14 *The promontory with the Late Bronze Age settlement of Palaeokastro-Maa, from the north-east.*
15 *Excavating the Late Bronze Age city wall of Kition.*
16 *Excavation of the Late Bronze Age city of Kition: structures of the late 13th century built on the collapsed roof of an earlier tomb.*
17 *Salamis, Tomb 3: impressions of the wooden parts of a chariot left in the soil of the dromos. 7th century B.C.*
18 *Excavating the Late Bronze Age city of Kition.*
19 *Salamis, Tomb 3: plaster cast from an impression of a chariot wheel. 7th century B.C.*
20 *Salamis, Tomb 79: impressions of the wooden parts of a chariot left in the soil of the dromos. Late 8th century B.C.*
21 *Salamis, Tomb 79: uncovering an ivory throne in the dromos. Late 8th century B.C.*

22 *Rectangular stone bowl from Khirokitia, with spout and handle. Height 4.5 cm., length 20.5 cm. Neolithic period.*

23 *Three necklaces of cornelian beads, steatite beads and dentalium shells, and a steatite fish amulet from Khirokitia. Length of amulet 4 cm. Neolithic period.*

24 *Combed Ware bowl from Khirokitia. Diameter 32.5 cm. Neolithic period.*

25 *Large White Painted pithos from Erimi. Height 53 cm. Chalcolithic period.*

26 *Neolithic burials from Khirokitia: platform with graves.*

27 *Detail of Plate 26.*

28 *General view of the Neolithic settlement of Sotira.*

29 *Neolithic burial from Khirokitia.*

30 *Clay head from Khirokitia. Height 10.5 cm. Neolithic period.*

31 *Neolithic stone bowl with relief decoration, from Khirokitia. Length 30.5 cm.*

32 *Steatite idol. Height 13.5 cm. Chalcolithic period.*

33 *Three idols of steatite, probably from the Paphos district. Height 5.6 cm., 9.3 cm., 5.7 cm. Chalcolithic period.*

34 *Two stone idols (one representing an animal's head, from Khirokitia). Height 10.5 cm. and 13.7 cm. respectively. Neolithic period.*

35 *Red Polished jug from Philia. Height 42 cm. Early Bronze Age.*

36 *Red Polished jug from Philia. Height 26 cm. Early Bronze Age.*

37 *Red Polished stemmed bowl with incised decoration; animal figures and small bowls on rim; from Vounous. Height 41 cm. Early Bronze Age.*

38 *Red Polished bowl with incised decoration and plastically rendered animal figures on the rim, from Vounous. Height 21.5 cm. Early Bronze Age.*

39 *Red Polished bowl with incised decoration and plastically rendered animal figures on the rim, from Vounous. Height 25 cm. Early Bronze Age.*

40 *Red Polished composite vase with incised decoration. Height 31 cm. Early Bronze Age.*

41 *Large Red Polished composite vase with incised decoration, from Vounous. Height 83 cm. Early Bronze Age.*

42 *White Polished (encrusted) gourd flask from Dhikomo. Height 32.5 cm. Early Bronze Age.*

43 *Large Red Polished jug decorated with patterns in relief, from Dhenia. Height 70 cm. Early Bronze Age.*

44 *Red-on-White bowl from Philia. Height 18 cm. Early Bronze Age.*

45 *Red Polished composite jug with incised decoration. Height 44 cm. Early Bronze Age.*

46 *Two Red Polished terracotta figurines of quadrupeds from Vounous. Height 9 cm. and 6 cm. respectively. Early Bronze Age.*

47 *Clay model of ploughing scene, from Vounous. Length 41 cm. Early Bronze Age.*

48 *Two quadrupeds in Red Polished and Black Polished ware respectively, with incised decoration. Height 13 cm. and 15 cm. respectively. Early Bronze Age.*

49 *Clay model of sacred enclosure from Vounous. Diameter 37 cm. Early Bronze Age.*

50 *Pair of gold hair ornaments, from Lapithos. Length 5.5 cm. Early Bronze Age.*

51 *Red Polished plank-shaped idol. Height 28 cm. Early Bronze Age.*

52 *Middle Minoan vase from Lapithos. Height 16.2 cm.*

53 *White Painted jug from Akhera. Height 25 cm. Beginning of Late Bronze Age.*

54 *Boat-shaped pyxis of White Painted ware, from Vounous. Height 23.7 cm. Middle Bronze Age.*

55 *Middle Minoan cup (Kamares ware) from Karmi. Height 9 cm.*

56 *Kition: rectangular tower built against the cyclopean wall, with a street running parallel to the city wall. Late Bronze Age.*

57 *General view of the area of the city wall, Kition. Late Bronze Age.*

58 *Mycenaean bowl from Kition, imitating a Cypriote shape. 13th century B.C.*

59 *Mycenaean rhyton in the Zeno Pierides Collection, Larnaca. Height 7 cm., length 20 cm. 13th century B.C.*

60 *Bronze ingot, from Enkomi. Length 74 cm. Late Bronze Age.*

61–62 *Impressions of two cylinder seals from Kition. Late Bronze Age.*

63 *Bird-shaped vase of Proto-White Painted Ware, from Salamis. 11th century B.C. (Expedition from University of Lyons).*

64 *Steatite Seal from Enkomi. Diameter 2.5 cm. Late Bronze Age.*

65 Bronze statue of a warrior god from Enkomi, standing on an ingot, wearing a horned helmet and greaves, and holding a shield and spear. Height 35 cm. (French Archaeological Expedition).

66 Proto-White Painted Ware kalathos, from Kouklia (Palaepaphos), decorated in the pictorial style. Height 15 cm., diameter 27 cm. 11th century B.C.

67 Ashlar block building, Enkomi ("Bâtiment 18"). Late Bronze Age.

68 The temple of the Horned God at Enkomi. Late Bronze Age.

69 Jug of Base Ring Ware, from Kantara. Height 46.5 cm. Late Bronze Age.

70 Mycenaean amphora decorated with human figures and bulls, from Enkomi. Height 46 cm. Early 14th century B.C.

71 Mycenaean crater decorated with a large bird chasing human figures in a chariot, from Enkomi. Height 32.5 cm. Early 14th century B.C.

72 Detail from a Mycenaean crater decorated with a chariot scene, from Pyla-Verghi. Early 14th century B.C.

73 Mycenaean bowls decorated with birds and fishes respectively, from Kition. Diameter 22 cm. and 20 cm. respectively. 13th century B.C.

74 Jug and bowl of White Slip Ware. Height 24 cm. and 16 cm. respectively.

75 Silver bowl decorated with bucrania in gold and niello, from Enkomi. Diameter 15.7 cm. 14th century B.C.

76–77 Two views of faience rhyton, from Kition; decorated with animal and human figures in red enamel or yellow and black paint on a blue enamel ground. Height 28 cm. 13th century B.C.

78 Terracotta figurine of a nude female figure (Mother Goddess). Height 21 cm. Late Bronze Age.

79 Terracotta figurine of a seated woman from Katydhata. Height 9.5 cm. Late Bronze Age.

80 Two gold finger-rings decorated with enamel, from Kouklia (Palaepaphos). Late Bronze Age.

81 Gold necklace with a cylinder-seal pendant of haematite from Ayios Iakovos and a gold pendant in the shape of a pomegranate, from Enkomi. Height of pendant 4.5 cm. Late Bronze Age.

82 Pair of gold ear-rings in the shape of bucrania, and a gold finger-ring with a paste bezel in the shape of a bucranium, from Kition. Length 2.7 cm. and 2.5 cm. respectively. Late Bronze Age.

83 *Gold pin with blue faience head, from Enkomi. Height 14 cm. Late Bronze Age.*

84 *Pair of gold boat-shaped ear-rings, from Kouklia (Palaepaphos). Late Bronze Age.*

85 *Long narrow bottle in variegated glass, from Arpera. Height 22.5 cm. Late Bronze Age.*

86 *Two gold necklaces, from Enkomi. Late Bronze Age.*

87 *Gold pectoral decorated with sphinxes in repoussé, from Enkomi. Length 17.5 cm. Late Bronze Age.*

88 *Two gold diadems decorated in repoussé, from Kition. Late Bronze Age.*

89 *Gold sceptre inlaid with enamel, from Kourion. Height 16.5 cm. Late Bronze Age (11th century B.C.).*

90 *Two alabaster vases, from Kition. Height 25 cm. and 18 cm. respectively. Late Bronze Age.*

91 *Two clay tablets inscribed in the Cypro-Minoan script, with a bone stylus. From Enkomi. Late Bronze Age.*

92 *Ivory handle of a mirror with representation in relief of a man attacking a lion, from Kouklia (Palaepaphos). Height 21.5 cm. Late Bronze Age.*

93 *Bronze tripod, from Amathus. Height 10 cm. Late Bronze Age.*

94 *Bronze statue of a god seated on a chair, from Enkomi. Height 15 cm. Late Bronze Age. (Paris, Louvre).*

95 *Bronze statue of the Horned God, from Enkomi. Height 54.5 cm. Late Bronze Age (12th century B.C.).*

96 *Mycenaean IIIC:1 bowl, from Sinda. Height 11.5 cm. Late Bronze Age (end of 13th century B.C.).*

97 *Bird vase of Proto-White Painted Ware, from Kouklia (Palaepaphos). Length 20 cm. Late Bronze Age (11th century B.C.).*

98 *Terracotta figurines, from Ayia Irini, Archaic period.*

99 *Terracotta group of a bull and two attendants, from Meniko. Height 28.5 cm. Archaic period.*

100 *Terracotta group of a chariot from Ayia Irini. and shield bearer. Archaic period.*

101 *Terracotta figurine of a female goddess, from near Morphou. Height 16 cm. Beginning of Iron Age.*

121 *Salamis, Tomb 79: bronze frontal band decorated with winged figures in relief of god El. Height 49.5 cm. End of 8th century B.C.*

122 *Salamis, Tomb 79: bronze figure of a soldier from the upper part of the linch-pin of a chariot wheel. Height 36 cm. End of 8th century B.C.*

123 *Salamis, Tomb 79: bronze standard from the yoke of a chariot. Height 50 cm. 7th century B.C.*

124 *Bronze horse's blinker decorated in relief with a lion attacking a bull, from Tomb 79, Salamis. Length 22 cm. Late 8th century B.C.*

125 *Bronze frontal band of a horse, from Tomb 47, Salamis. Height 38 cm. 7th century B.C.*

126 *Bronze incense-burner from Angolemi. Height 28.5 cm. Archaic period.*

127 *Salamis, Tomb 79: ivory plaque with a sphinx cut out and inlaid with paste. Height 16 cm. Late 8th century B.C.*

128 *Salamis, Tomb 79: ivory plaque with a composite lotus flower cut out and inlaid with paste. Height 16.2 cm. Late 8th century B.C.*

129 *Salamis, Tomb 79: ivory plaques decorated with sphinxes in relief and gilded with thin gold leaves. Height 7 cm. Late 8th century B.C.*

130 *Salamis, Tomb 79: ivory plaques decorated with a seated god in relief with the ankh symbol hanging from a palm tree, gilded with thin gold leaves. Height 7 cm. Late 8th century B.C.*

131 *Salamis, Tomb 79: an ivory incense-burner. Height 31 cm. Late 8th century B.C.*

132 *Iron sword, with silver studded hilt, from Tomb 3, Salamis. Length 92.5 cm. Late 7th century B.C.*

133 *Salamis, Tomb 79: two ivory plaques decorated with floral pattern in relief and inlaid with blue glass. Height 18.5 cm. and 21.5 cm. Late 8th century B.C.*

134 *Salamis, Tomb 79: ivory throne from the dromos. Height 90 cm. End of 8th century B.C.*

135 *Gold diadem decorated in repoussé with a chariot scene, from Tomb 31, Salamis. Length 9.5 cm. 7th century B.C.*

136 *Necklace of gold and rock-crystal beads, from Tomb 1, Salamis. End of 8th century B.C.*

137 *Terracotta figurines (bearded figure, rosettes, pomegranates, beads, etc.) from a pyre at Cellarka, Salamis. 6th century B.C.*

138 *Bronze cow from the temple of Athena, Vouni Palace. Classical period, 5th century B.C. Length 19 cm.*

139 *View of the Palace of Vouni. Courtyard and megaron, from the north-east. Classical period.*

140 *Bronze relief representing two lions attacking a bull, from the temple of Athena, Vouni Palace. Length 23.5 cm. Classical period. 5th century B.C.*

141 *Pair of gold bracelets. Diameter 4.6 cm. Classical period.*

142 *Interior of royal tomb at Tamassos, imitating wooden architecture. 6th century B.C.*

143 *Entrance of a royal tomb at Tamassos with a Cypriote capital at the entrance. 6th century B.C.*

144 *White Painted Ware jug with moulded figures on the shoulder, from Marion. Height 42.5 cm.*

145 *Terracotta stand made up of two opposed female figures, from Tomb 47, Salamis. Height 27 cm. 7th century B.C.*

146 *Two amphorae of variegated glass. Height 15 cm. and 16 cm. respectively. Hellenistic period.*

147 *Stemmed bowl in polychrome ware, with female figures in relief round the stem, from Tomb 23, Salamis. 7th century B.C. Height 22.5 cm.*

148 *Salamis necropolis: general view of rock-cut tombs at Cellarka (7th-4th centuries B.C.).*

149 *Pyre with offerings outside a tomb at Cellarka, 6th century B.C.*

150 *Bronze head of Zeus Ammon with eyeballs inlaid with silver, from Soloi. Height 5 cm. Hellenistic period.*

151 *Pair of gold ear-rings. Height 3.5 cm. Hellenistic period.*

152 *Salamis, Tomb 77: carbonised almonds, grapes and cereals. End of 4th century B.C.*

153 *Salamis, Tomb 77: three gilded alabastra. Height 23 cm. End of 4th century B.C.*

154 *Salamis, Tomb 77: the tumulus before excavation. End of 4th century B.C.*

155 *Salamis, Tomb 77: the rectangular exedra under the tumulus with the mound of stones on top of the pyre. End of 4th century B.C.*

156 *Salamis, Tomb 77: the top of the exedra with the pyre in the centre. End of 4th century B.C.*

157 *Kato Paphos: a rock-cut "royal" tomb of the Hellenistic period. Colonnaded courtyard in front of the chamber.*

158 *Salamis, Tomb 77: clay female head on the pyre on floor of exedra. End of 4th century B.C.*

159 *Chalcedony gem from Salamis, signed by its engraver Hyllos. 2.2 × 1.5 cm. Early Roman Imperial period.*

160 *Silver stater of uncertain king, Soloi (?). 5th century B.C.*

161 *Silver stater of a king of Idalion.*

162 *Silver stater of King Timocharis of Marion (2nd half of 5th to beginning of 4th century B.C.). Head of Apollo.*

163 *Silver stater of King Evagoras I of Salamis (411–374 B.C.). Head of bearded Heracles wearing lion's skin.*

164 *Limestone portrait head. Height 25 cm. Early 1st century A.D.*

165 *Marble head of Aphrodite, from Salamis. Height 32 cm. 4th century B.C.*

166 *Limestone relief representing a bearded head of Dionysus, from Mathiati. Height 51.5 cm. Hellenistic period.*

167 *General view of Kato Paphos harbour, from the north-east.*

168 *Part of the aqueduct of Salamis near the village of Ayios Serghios. Late Roman period.*

169 *Salamis, the gymnasium: the east stoa of the palaestra, seen from the south. Late Roman period.*

170 *Salamis, the gymnasium: in the foreground the latrines, in the background the palaestra of the gymnasium. Late Roman period. View from the north, west.*

171 *Salamis, Tomb 77: clay head of King Nicocreon (?). Height 17 cm. End of 4th century B.C.*

172 *Marble head of a woman, from Kourion. Height 25 cm. Hellenistic period (early 3rd century B.C.).*

173 *Salamis, the gymnasium: fresco in a niche above the south entrance of the central sudatorium, representing Hylas and the nymph. End of 3rd century A.D.*

174 *Salamis, the gymnasium: in the foreground the north annexe with statues surrounding a swimming pool, in the background supporting half-arches against the north wall of the north sudatorium. Late Roman period.*

Photographs Nos 4, 5, 9, 10, 15–21, 26–32, 56–66, 75, 113–123, 142, 143, 148, 149, 154–163 and 166–168 by the Department of Antiquities, Nicosia.
All other photos by Gérard Bertin, Geneva.

INDEX

(The numbers in italics refer to illustrations).

Printed in Switzerland

THE TEXT AND ILLUSTRATIONS
IN THIS VOLUME WERE PRINTED
ON THE PRESSES OF NAGEL
PUBLISHERS IN GENEVA

FINISHED IN JANUARY 1969
BINDING BY NAGEL PUBLISHERS,
GENEVA

PLATES ENGRAVED BY CLICHÉS UNION,
PARIS

LEGAL DEPOSIT No 463

PRINTED IN SWITZERLAND

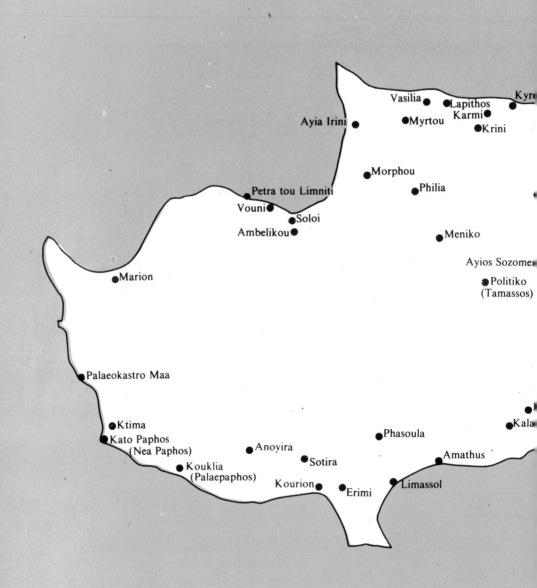

Vasilia · · Lapithos Kyr...
Ayia Irini · · Myrtou Karmi ·
· Krini

Morphou ·
· Philia

Petra tou Limniti
Vouni · · Meniko
· Soloi
Ambelikou ·

Ayios Sozome...

Marion · · Politiko
(Tamassos)

Palaeokastro Maa

· Kala...

Ktima · · Phasoula
Kato Paphos · Anoyira
(Nea Paphos) · · Amathus
Kouklia · Sotira
(Palaepaphos) Kourion · · Erimi · Limassol